101

Ways to Be a Terrific
Sports Parent

● ●

Making Athletics a Positive
Experience for Your Child

DR. JOEL FISH

WITH SUSAN MAGEE

A Fireside Book
Published by Simon & Schuster
New York London Toronto Sydney

FIRESIDE
Rockefeller Center
1230 Avenue of the Americas
New York, NY 10020

For information about special discounts for bulk purchases,
please contact Simon & Schuster Special Sales:
1-800-456-6798 or business@simonandschuster.com

Designed by Jaime Putorti

Manufactured in the United States of America

10   9   8   7   6   5   4

Library of Congress Cataloging-in-Publication Data
   Fish, Joel.
101 ways to be a terrific sports parent : making athletics a positive
experience for your child / Joel Fish with Susan Magee.
     p.   cm.
"A Fireside book."
Includes index.
1. Sports for children—Psychological aspects. 2. Parenting—
Psychological aspects. I. Title: One hundred one ways to be a terrific
sports parent. II. Title: One hundred and one ways to be a terrific sports
parent. III. Magee, Susan. IV. Title.
GV709.2.F534 2003
796'.083—dc21   2003050462

ISBN 978-0-7432-2702-5
ISBN 0-7432-2702-6

To my father, Dr. Edward Fish, of blessed memory, who taught me so much about love, appreciating life, and parenting.

To my mother, Sara Fish, who has taught me the meaning of unconditional love.

To my wife Deborah, and my children Eli, Ari, and Talia, who are the greatest joys in my life.

To my brother, Dr. Neal Fish, who is the best sibling a brother could have.

Contents

. . . .

Introduction

. . . .

Why our sports-playing kids need our help

Today, a record number of kids play sports—approximately 40 million boys and girls, ages 6-17. That's a lot of sports-playing kids *and* a lot of sports parents.

If you're reading this book, you are most likely the parent of one or more of these kids. You, like many other sports parents today, may have a question, issue, or concern about your sports-playing child.

If you do, I promise you, you're not alone.

As a licenced psychologist and sport psychologist with over 20 years of clinical experience dealing with a wide range of athletes, both professional and amateur, I have met and worked with many parents. In fact, I meet parents every day who tell me they feel confused, stressed out, or simply unsure of how to deal with the many issues and pressures raised by their child playing a sport. These are hardworking, caring moms and dads from all backgrounds, walks of life, and income levels who have lots of questions—lots and lots of them—but few answers when it comes to helping their kids have a positive sports experience.

I routinely hear questions from concerned parents like:

My child seems quieter since joining the soccer team. Could he be stressed out?

My daughter's field hockey coach pushes very hard; is this okay?

Our son seems totally disinterested in sports. Should we sign him up anyway?

My daughter wants to quit the swim team mid-season. Will letting her quit send a bad message?

I'm a single mom raising a teenage son. He seems obsessed with winning. Is this just normal "boy" behavior?

Our eleven-year-old daughter is into skateboarding but we worry that there's an unhealthy subculture that goes with it. Is this true?

Today's Sports Parents Are Often in Uncharted Territory

It's no wonder that some parents feel they have more questions than answers. Youth sports have changed quite a bit over the years, but especially in the last twenty years. Sports parents today often find themselves in uncharted territory.

When I was a kid (I'm 48 years old now), after school or during the summer, I just walked out the back door, grabbed a baseball or hockey stick, and headed out to the street or to a nearby field to find some other kids to play with. We played for hours with no uniforms, no refs, no parents on the sidelines urging us to victory. Sure, I liked to win; we all did. But if we didn't it wasn't the end of the world. We thought, "We'll get them next time."

We played for hours. We played until the sky became so dark we couldn't see the ball anymore. We played until our mothers had to force us back inside. We played hard because we loved to play. It was fun.

Then, kids who played sports were just playing games, often with whoever was available from the neighborhood or playground. Now, kids who play sports are highly organized on teams and in leagues. Few kids are let out of the door and sent off to play or left to their own devices. There is far less spontaneous play. Now, kids are coached, trained, conditioned, and judged. Most youth sports occur on teams or in leagues—there are fewer and fewer pickup games. Back when we were kids, if we played on a team, it was most likely a school team and we played for the school year and then we stopped. Now there are school teams that end but recreational leagues, after-school leagues, intramural sports, weekend leagues, summer leagues, sport camps, and year-round travel teams that go on and on.

Today, there are sports and competitions for things that weren't even considered sports when you were a kid—in-line skating, snowboarding, downhill racing, and skateboarding. The range of sports today is incredibly diverse.

I'm sure you don't need me to tell you that youth sports today are not like when you were a kid—you're living it. You're the one out there juggling schedules, shuttling your child to practices, attending the games and shelling out the money for uniforms and equipment.

There's Lots of Good in Youth Sports Today—But . . .

In many ways, the changes that have occurred in youth sports since you were young are extremely positive. The sheer volume of kids playing sports today is terrific. It used to be that only the talented kids could play on teams; now kids of all skill levels can participate and that's good news for everybody. One of the reasons the number of sports-playing kids has skyrocketed is because the opportunities for girls to play sports has exploded in the last twenty-five years. In fact, one out of three sports-playing kids today is a girl. Kids can also participate now at younger ages. It used to be only school-aged kids had the chance to play organized sports. In general, kids of all ages, everywhere, have the opportunity to play more kinds of sports than ever before.

All great things. But there is a downside to all the changes in youth sports today.

Though a record forty million kids are playing sports, too many of them are unhappy. In fact, over 30 percent of them are quitting, dropping out, and throwing in the towel by the time they're thirteen!

The reason?

According to studies conducted by the Youth Sport Institute at Michigan State University, the majority of kids who quit sports say it's because they're not having any fun. Kids today feel too much pressure to win.

Think about that for a minute. That's nearly twelve million kids who were not having any fun playing soccer, basketball, hockey, tennis, and many other sports. Twelve million kids! That's a lot of kids who become disenchanted with sports. The sports-playing kids I work with often tell me they feel stressed out, worried, and overwhelmed. Something is very wrong. Sports is supposed to be fun! Once, not so long ago, it *was* fun.

In today's highly organized and specialized youth sports environment, more and more sports-playing kids feel that just giving their best during a game or competition is not good enough. At younger and younger ages, kids are sent the message: "If you don't win, don't play. Winning is the reason we play. Winning is everything."

When winning is everything, the competitive environment can become a stressful and negative place for youngsters.

When winning is everything, sports is no longer fun.

What Sports Can Mean for Your Child in the Long Run

The high dropout rate in youth sports does not just hold short-term consequences for your child. The experiences we have as children playing sports help shape us as adults. For better or for worse, our early sports experience leaves its mark upon us. Athletics is one of the arenas in which, as children, we develop our identities. Self-esteem and self-confidence issues are frequently raised. A child with a poor athletic image and little confidence in sports may feel bad about him- or herself for years to come. The memories your child will have from the big game, the big race, the tournament, often stick to them like glue. Even events that happen at routine practices and games can profoundly influence your child for years to come, like getting laughed at or teased by teammates and how they are treated by coaches. I work with many adults, including professional athletes, and I can tell you that the memories we carry with us from sports are powerful ones. I know because adults frequently share their memories with me. Sports memories are typically vivid; the emotions attached to them are surprisingly fresh and often quite painful.

If your child is quitting sports, or is at risk to quit later, because she isn't having fun, whatever negative experience she has had may well follow her through adulthood. That's certainly not good. If your child drops out of sports, he won't reap the many benefits that sports has to offer—like goal setting, perseverance, teamwork, and fitness. That's not good either.

Why Sports Parents Make All the Difference

Parents frequently ask me, "How can I make sure that my child has a good experience in sports? What's the secret?"

Some parents believe the secret is finding the right coach. Others say it's all in how she gets along with her teammates. Still others believe the secret is to match him with the sport that best fits his personality and temperament.

Yes, coaches, teammates, and the sport he plays matter. But the most critical factor in whether the forty million sports-playing children love their sports experiences or hate them is the behavior—both public and private—and the attitude of their parents. This fact surprises many parents.

Certainly, outside people and outside factors matter, and yes, these outside influences do contribute to shaping your child. But there's no doubt about it—parents always have had, and always will have, the most significant influence over their kids. What you think about your child is more important to him than what anyone else thinks. If your daughter feels, "Mom and Dad are proud of me," that is more significant than acceptance from a coach or peer. But if your child feels, or even gets a hint, that Mom and Dad love me more when I play well or when I win, then that puts her under a lot of pressure. Kids who feel too much pressure to win don't enjoy sports. These are the kids who either quit youth sports or wish they could.

101 Ways to Be a Terrific Sports Parent

In addition to my work as a licensed psychologist and sport psychologist, I'm also a dad. My wife Debbie and I have three children (Eli, age fourteen, and twins, Talia and Ari, age ten) who play sports. From both my professional and personal experience, I can tell you that parenting a child in sports today can often be challenging—sometimes very challenging!

I'd like to help make sports parenting a little less challenging for you. Moms and dads tell me that having the right information about their child's emotional and physical needs in sports, combined with some inspiration, helps a lot when they find themselves in that sometimes complex and confusing world of youth sports. Throughout this book you will find 101 ways to help your child be successful on and off the field. Some of these 101 ways will encourage you to take specific action steps regarding your role as a sports parent. Others will just ask you to consider a piece of advice or information. You certainly don't have to memorize these key points or read them and digest them all at once. Some may apply to an experience you and your child may be having now or maybe not for another ten years. Keep in mind, your ten-year-old soccer or hockey maniac may become the fourteen-year-old you have to force to go to practice. As you'll discover, the age of your child matters in how you'll deal with various issues. This is why throughout this book I generally break age down into three general categories. Elementary school–age (six-to-eleven-year old) kids tend to see things in black and white terms. They need help finding the gray areas. Middle school–age kids (twelve to fourteen years old) begin to wrestle with identity issues. They're asking, "Who am I?" and we need to help them find a positive answer.

During the high school years (fifteen years old and up), peer pressure sets in and kids need our help to make the best choices for themselves.

You may already be aware of, or putting into practice, many of these important sports-parenting guidelines—whether you know it or not. Many parents are doing a great job parenting their sports-playing kids. Sometimes parents say to me, "Well, I'm just happy to know I am doing the right thing." Reassurance can mean a lot when we're trying to parent our children in sports. If your child is happy in sports there's no reason why he or she can't stay that way—especially once you have read this book, which is packed full of tips, techniques, and advice for parenting your child in sports at every age.

Or, you may be reading this with the full knowledge that your child is not having a good time in sports and you're wondering what, if anything, you can do about it. I ask you not to worry either. As you'll discover throughout this book, there's plenty you can do about it. You *can* help your child have a better experience in sports. I've worked with many families having issues and problems with their sports-playing children and just about all of them were able to resolve them, often quickly, and sometimes even easily. But before that can happen, you need to understand what your child is truly experiencing out there on the field, the court, or the playground.

I offer these 101 ways to be a terrific sports parent to you because the parents I have worked with and spoken to throughout the years have told me that this is the information they find most helpful and useful. These are the guidelines that help create terrific sports parents and happy and healthy sports-playing kids. I'm confident it can help you and your sports-playing child.

In sports, you cannot script the outcome of events. You can't always get what you want. We cannot guarantee that our sports-playing kids will have a good time or a good experience. We cannot guarantee that as parents we won't make some mistakes. But I can promise you this: If you are knowledgeable and aware of what your child is experiencing emotionally and physically in sports, you will be better able to give your child what he or she needs in order to have a good experience. When sports-playing kids get what they need from their parents—the right kind of love, support, guidance, and encouragement—they will stick with sports and reap many benefits for years to come. And when that happens, everyone wins.

I

. . . .

AWARENESS:

Why you're the most important influence

Today, more than ever, sports-playing kids need their parents to be aware of the many pressures and challenges they face on the playing field—including a relentless pressure to win that most parents themselves didn't experience. Sports-playing kids need moms and dads to be aware of their own motivations and desires, which influence them as sports parents.

Here are eleven ways you can become more aware of what kind of sports parent you are and what your child needs from you the most:

1. Give your child unconditional love, no matter what happens on the field

You buy your child the shoes and the uniform she needs to play soccer. You send your son to a three-week summer football clinic so he can improve his game. You offer her advice on how to improve her backhand. You drive him to 6 A.M. ice hockey practice. You give your time after work and on the weekends to help her practice her pitching. But are you giving her what she *really* needs to be successful and happy in sports?

Today's sports parents give their young athletes so much— time, money, and energy—more than most of our parents gave to us. It's not that our parents didn't love us or didn't care, it's just that today's parents are more involved in all of their children's activities, including sports. More parents attend their children's sporting events than ever before—that's clear just by looking at the stands. Parents know more about the sports their kids are playing. They are more actively involved in making decisions about coaching, strategy, and which games their children will play. A child's sports activities are built into the structure of his or her parents' day or, for working parents, their weekends. As one mom of three teenage boys put it, "On the weekends, I should just put my coffeemaker in the mini van and sleep there."

The motive behind the increased involvement as sports parents is a good one. Parents want to give their children the best opportunities in sports. More parental involvement can certainly be positive for children. Kids love their parents' attention. They love to be supported by Mom and Dad. But I believe, very passionately, because I have witnessed it time and time again in my work with families, that although many very good, hardworking parents are putting in a lot of time, effort, and money to nurture their children in sports, too many kids are still not getting what they need. *What young athletes need the most is unconditional love and support from Mom or Dad no matter what happens on the field or on the playground.*

Instead of unconditional love, too many kids are getting pressure—pressure to win, pressure to excel, pressure to make the all-star team, pressure to make Mom and Dad proud.

Toby, an eleven-year-old ice hockey player, told me, "Dr. Fish, my dad gets so excited when I win I don't want him to be mad at me if I don't."

Now, I've met Toby's dad several times and he's a nice guy. He doesn't yell at Toby or cajole him to perform better from the bleachers. When Toby wins, sure he claps and shouts, "Great job, Toby!" When Toby messes up on the ice, his dad is quick to tell him, "Shake it off, buddy! Don't worry about it!"

So why in the world would this boy think his dad would be mad at him?

As parents, we know how much we love our kids. Sure, we can be disappointed in them sometimes. We get frustrated with our kids. We get angry. These feelings, though uncomfortable to experience, are totally normal. Emotions run high in sports for everybody, including parents. But underneath those temporary feelings of disappointment or anger are feelings of love. Of course!

But kids don't automatically know this. Your child doesn't understand that you have this great reservoir of love for her that will never get used up. She doesn't always know that feelings, like anger and disappointment if she blows it on the tennis court, are temporary but that your love for her is not. Though we know our love is not conditional, kids think that it is. They see or sense our anger, disapproval, and disappointment and they get scared. They think, "Wow, Dad is really upset. I really let him down. I don't think he loves me anymore."

Kids need to be constantly reminded of the love and positive feelings we have toward them. This goes for kids of all ages. High school age kids will try to convince you that they don't care what you think, but they do. We must reassure them that our love for them is not based on how well they do on the field or court. We must tell them, again and again, that yes, we like when they win, because it's fun to win, it feels good to win, but we love them win or lose no matter what. Become a broken record with the message: "I love you when you win. I love you just as much when you lose." With the pressure and the competition sports-playing kids now face, you really can't say it enough.

You can show your unconditional love with hugs, by running your hand through his hair, by holding her hand when she's leaving the field (though don't try this on your twelve- or thirteen-year-old), or another gesture of tenderness you feel is appropriate to your child. One dad bought his son an ice cream cone after every game but he got a double dip when he lost.

Reassure your boy that you love him win *or* lose. Tell him, "It's great that you won, but even if you'd lost the game or dropped the ball, you still would have been my champ." It's important to remind kids that even though we're happy and excited when they do well in sports, it's okay when they don't do well, too. We still love them. You have more credibility with your child when you say, "I love you," when they win *and* when they don't. Then they think, "Mom must really mean it if she's saying it now *and* when I lose."

2. Talk to your children about their experiences in sports

We hear a lot about why sports is good for kids—the exercise, the discipline, the fun. But here's another benefit you may not have thought about—sports gives you an opportunity to talk with your boy or girl.

This may not seem like much of a benefit to you now if your child is still under the age of eleven or twelve. Young children love to talk to their parents and share their experiences. Sure, you have to drag information out of them on occasion, but you know how to eventually get them talking. However, as your child ages, you may find that sports will be one of the few areas that you still have in common. Clarisse told me that if her sixteen-year-old Michaela didn't play lacrosse, she probably would never talk to her daughter:

> *Michaela thinks I don't understand her struggles at school, with her friends, and boys. When I express interest, she rolls her eyes and says, "You don't get it, Mom." Maybe I don't understand other things in her life, but I do get lacrosse strategy. I've been driving her to games and practices for three years. We talk about how she did in the game, what frustrated her, and what she's happy about. She tells me about her coach and stories about the other girls on the team. Sometimes we laugh at something that happened. The point is, we talk. Talking to Michaela about sports is just easier than talking to her about the other areas of her life. It's our common ground.*

Here are four guidelines you can use for getting the conversation about sports started and keeping it going:

- **Check in weekly.** Sports should be one of the things you ask your child about on a regular basis. Kids want their parents to be interested in everything they do. The biggest mistake is not that parents don't talk to their kids, it's that they tend to tune in the most when there's a problem. Don't let the ordinary moments pass you by; they are ripe with opportunities to learn something new about your boy or girl or just enjoy each other's company. Tune in and make time to talk, even after the uneventful game or practice. You don't have to have a major talk after every sporting event, practice, or game but try to get in the habit of at least having a weekly conversation with your boy or girl. You can simply ask, "How is soccer going?" or "Anything exciting going on in field hockey?" When parents view and approach sports as one more opportunity to learn about their children and to talk to them about another area of their lives, both kids and parents benefit. An ongoing dialogue about sports keeps you in tune with what your child is thinking and allows your child to hear your point of view. Parents tell me that they learn so much about their kids by talking to them about sports. One dad said, "I didn't know that Marcus was so aware of other people's feelings. He can tell when his coach is upset or when one of his teammates needs some encouragement. That's pretty good for a nine-year-old."

- **Listen more than you talk.** Parents with happy sports-playing kids do more listening than talking. They ask open-ended questions that encourage talk rather than a simple yes or no answer. They ask: "How do you feel about Coach?" "How can I help you enjoy hockey more?" or "You seem to be enjoying soccer so much this season. How come?" Then they are quiet and they let their kids do the talking. Part of the reason that parents don't listen enough is that they feel they have to solve their child's problems for them. As Teresa put it: "I can't stand to see Marissa hurting if one of her teammates says something mean. I used to try to devise strategies for her or help her think of what to say but within thirty seconds she'd be turning up the radio to drown me out. Now I've learned to say, 'That must have really hurt your feelings when Sally said you blew it,' and then let her talk about it." I know a mom who had to count to ten each time she had the urge to jump in and add something to what her son was saying. If you practice, listening more than you talk becomes a habit.

- **Be a parent and not a coach.** Don't center the conversation around what your daughter did wrong or how she could have done better. Kids are much more likely to talk to you if you point out what they did well. You can say, "I know you're disappointed that you didn't get a hit, but we're going to keep practicing. I really loved your effort today. And I saw that terrific play you made at second base." I know it's hard not to give advice or feedback, especially when you know that if your son relaxed his shoulders when he pitched, he'd perform better. I have to bite my tongue too. It's hard for any parent not to try to solve your child's problems. It's fine that you want to help your boy or girl achieve in athletics but remember that unless you're the one with the whistle and the clipboard drilling the team every Saturday, you're not a coach. (Parents who are their child's coach can find advice in Coaching Concerns, chapter 5). Kids need their moms and dads to be the cheerleader who always listens and, on occasion, gives good advice.

- **Talk about sports in a nonathletic environment.** If you find your child reluctant to talk to you about his sports experiences after a practice or a game, don't worry. It doesn't mean you have bad communication or that your child is hiding something from you. Sammy, a twelve-year-old youth football player told me, "Dr. Fish, I don't always want to talk about football right after I play. I get sick of it. I want my dad to talk to me about other stuff, like school or the soap box derby we're going to enter." This is very common. Kids get burned out on sports and need to recharge. Think about how you feel after work or after you've come home from the PTA meeting. Do you always want to talk about your day or what you talked about? Sometimes you just want to get your mind off your daily activities. Kids are the same way. Give them a chance to decompress from their practice or game. Pick a comfortable spot for your child, like her bedroom or the kitchen. Wait until you're playing Monopoly, tossing a ball, or doing the dishes before engaging her in conversation. You're likely to find that your child will be more willing to open up about sports if she's away from the source of the conflict.

3. Remember the reasons to play sports outside of winning

Kids learn early on that winning in sports is what counts. They see that if you win, you get a coveted spot on the all-star team. If you win, Mom and Dad are proud. If you win, your peers admire you and Coach is happy. You get the trophies; you're a champ. But if you don't win, you disappoint everyone.

Kids learn that winning is what counts from the media too. Our TVs routinely beam us pictures of the stars, like Tiger Woods and Michael Jordan, the athletes who have "made it." The sports media focuses on the champs, the winners, and the top dogs rather than the teams. Kids hear about professional players making millions of dollars and know they are admired for it. Kids of all ages are truly spellbound by larger than life sports heroes. Twenty years ago, if you asked a ten-year-old boy, "Who is your hero?" he probably would have named an astronaut, the President, or a superhero character. Today, he would probably say, "Michael Jordan," or another professional athlete. Millions of young girls admire basketball player Sue Bird and ice skater Michelle Kwan.

It's easy to get caught up in the idea that winning is what counts most in sports when it's all around you, on the field and coming out of the television. When we focus on winning we forget the many reasons why it's good for kids to play sports. When I was a kid, I liked to win, but I also liked hanging out with the other boys on my team. It was a lot of fun. I can remember feeling strong and vital when I played sports. I liked being out in the fresh air. Looking back now, I realize that I was probably more self-confident and self-assured as a teenager because I played sports.

Fun, fitness, fresh air, commitment, camaraderie, team-work, perseverance, goal setting, the thrill of competition, and enhanced self-esteem . . . these are all the reasons why I encourage my children to play sports. I'm sure these are the reasons why you want your children to play sports too. The problem is, with so much attention paid to all-star teams, scores, and standings, it's easy to forget the many great reasons to play sports outside of winning. I struggle with this too. When I'm in the bleachers watching my son Eli play football and it's 7–7 with one minute left in the last quarter, it's hard to remember that I'm glad Eli's there because it's fun. I have to sit on my hands and bite my tongue pretty hard when the other team intercepts the ball. I have to remind myself that winning is only one small part of the whole sports picture. I make a conscious effort to talk to my kids at least two or three times a season about all the good reasons to play sports. I'll ask, "Not counting the championship game, what was the best thing about playing soccer this season?"

If one of my kids is playing for a particularly competitive coach or some of the other parents are pushing the kids to win, I remind them about the other reasons to play sports. Before or after every game. I'll say, "Yeah, Ari, I know it's hard when you don't win, but you sure looked like you were having fun with Jordan and Tory out there."

Though coaches, peers, and the media do influence your child about the importance of winning, parents have the most influence. If you take an early and proactive approach and remind both yourself and your child on a regular basis that winning isn't the only reason to play sports, you can help your child have a better experience in youth sports.

4. Beware of going overboard

Let me clarify what I mean by "overboard" or "overinvolved" parents. I don't mean the rare parent who totally loses control and punches a referee or even worse. Thankfully, the incidents of outright violent remain on the fringe.

I do mean the ever-increasing number of parents who are "crossing a line" every day with behaviors such as yelling at kids, screaming at coaches, arguing with officials, and/or cheating. Go to any community in the country and you can find examples of sports parents losing control. Yelling and screaming at a coach, fighting with other parents, and arguing with officials are the most obvious indications that you're an overboard or overinvolved sports parent.

Here are eight common signs that you're overboard as a sports parent. You:

✓ find yourself talking more about your child's sport than your child.

✓ are highly critical of your child's coach.

✓ talk to your child more like a coach than a parent (i.e., always giving advice, instruction, and critiques).

✓ constantly tell your child to practice more.

✓ seem more emotionally invested in the sport than your child (i.e., you get more upset than he or she does about a lost game or performance mistake).

✓ get a great deal of status and prestige from your child's athletic accomplishments.

✓ believe that if your child just tried harder he or she could be successful at sports.

✓ aren't hearing what your child is telling you (i.e., "Mom, I don't like when you stand behind me and tell me what to do." Or "Dad, it makes me nervous when you come to my games").

If you see yourself in any of the above, it's likely that you're going overboard in your child's sporting career. Please understand, you are not a terrible parent. I believe that many overboard sports parents sincerely are trying to help their kids or advocate for them. Many overboard sports parents regret their behavior later. Many of them tell me, "I just couldn't help myself."

Of course you can help yourself. You're an adult. You have control over your behavior.

But before you can change your behavior, you have to be aware of what you're doing and saying; otherwise you will continue to make the same mistakes over and over again. Be willing to look at your own behavior. Be willing to change. This is why your awareness as a sports parent is so critical.

5. Watch out for "blind spots" in your behavior

Having blind spots is a fact of human behavior and can be especially common in sports parenting because emotions run so high, because moms and dads are putting out a lot of effort, and because the competitive environment is supercharged. Even the most loving and caring parents can have blind spots. We all have them. We're not always tuned in; we don't always have the most accurate view of our own behavior.

By now you may be saying to yourself, "Well, I must be the exception here because I really and truly don't care if my son wins or loses the track meet." Or "I still love my daughter just as much, even if she doesn't score a lot of points during her basketball game. I would never let her think otherwise."

Of course you love your child no matter what happens during a game or on the field. In your heart you sincerely mean this—most parents do feel this way. But in the heat of the moment, are you absolutely sure this is what you're communicating to your child? In the car after a lost game or at dinner later that evening, are you certain you're acting like everything is fine?

Edward was absolutely, positively certain that he was sending his son Jacob a positive message of unconditional love and support. During one of our meetings, Edward swore up and down that he would never make his eleven-year-old son feel bad for not swimming well. "I love Jacob unconditionally," he said. "I don't really care if he wins or loses. I would never yell at him like some other parents yell at their kids."

Just then Jacob looked up and said, "Then how come when

I swim well you talk a lot in the car but if I have a bad meet, you stare out the window and don't say a word?"

Edward was stunned. He had no idea he was communicating his disappointment to his son this way. This is actually quite common—parents often have no idea what they're really doing and saying when it comes to their kids and sports. The way we respond to and act toward our sports-playing children can become habit-forming, the way it was for Jacob's dad. When it came to sports, he had a "blind spot" to how he was feeling, thinking, or behaving. His behavior was obvious to everyone else, but because he had so much emotion invested in sports and seeing Jacob succeed in swimming, he couldn't be objective about his own actions.

I encouraged Edward to check in with Jacob for periodic reality checks about his attitudes and behavior about sports. He now regularly asks his son: "So, how am I doing as a sports dad? Is there anything you think I should know? Is there anything I'm doing that's bothering you?"

Checking in with your child works only if you're willing to listen to what your child is telling you. You can't listen if you're talking, so hear your child out. It's okay to clarify what your child is telling you, such as, "What you're telling me is I'm still making you nervous when I come to your games" or "You feel like I'm still talking about sports too much." Clarify but don't argue. And don't try to talk your child out of how he feels by saying something like, "But I didn't even cheer or say one word when I was at your game." If your child is telling you that your behavior is causing a problem, it most likely is.

Also, be sure to check in with your spouse or your child's other parent, or a person who knows you and your child. Ask, "I'm not sure how I'm doing in keeping a balanced attitude about Lisa's lacrosse. What do you think?" Friends, other family members, like grandparents, and coaches can also give you an objective opinion and reality check about your behavior and attitudes as a sports parent. But no matter whom you turn to for help, you have to be willing to hear the truth—and that's not always easy. Remember to keep an open mind. Remind yourself that hearing the truth will help you discover any blind spots you may have as a sports parent.

6. Acknowledge that sports is emotional for you

A mom and dad are at their daughter's soccer match. They watch excitedly as their daughter cleverly maneuvers the ball away from the other team's player and approaches the goal. The goalie for the other team looks scared. Their daughter is going to make her first goal of the season! Suddenly, just as she's about to launch the ball, the referee blows his whistle. Mom and Dad watch in horror as he calls a foul on their daughter.

Suddenly the dad finds himself up and running onto the field to confront the referee. His face is red and his fists are clenched. The coach has to come out and ask this parent to please sit down.

Time for a confession: That dad described above was me about two years ago at my daughter Talia's soccer game. The coach who made me sit down was all of eighteen years old. Not a pleasant experience or memory for any sports dad, but imagine being a trained sport psychologist on top of that! Afterward, I was humiliated. It was a downright humbling experience.

Now, when I speak to parents' groups I share this embarrassing and painful memory. I do because it helps the audience understand how easy it is for a parent—even when he or she knows better—to lose control of his emotions when it comes to his sports-playing child.

I'm my own best example.

Going overboard by running out onto the field, while I'm not proud of it, has at least taught me a really good lesson—parents need help handling the emotions that sports generates just as much as kids do.

Why is this true? Why are sports often an emotional hotbed for parents? Why do so many otherwise normal, loving, mild-mannered moms and dads turn into tigers when it comes to their kids and sports?

Watching your child play sports, especially when the environment is very competitive, can be nerve-racking. Just sitting in the stands during those game-defining moments can be emotionally draining for moms and dads.

It's one thing to say, "It's okay if Becky doesn't get a hit," when the score is 10–4. But when it's all tied up and the bases are loaded, you do want Becky to get a hit. You want your daughter to be the winner, the hero. If she gets a hit and the umpire makes a questionable foul call, you'll react—whether it's internally or externally. You will feel a lot of emotion.

These are the kinds of moments when the game is not intellectual; it's emotional.

These are the moments that some parents, who are normally polite, in-control people, go overboard and start yelling from the stands.

These are the moments when Mom or Dad runs onto the field and gets in an umpire's or a coach's face and starts arguing.

When we see our kids being treated unfairly we react. When our kids make mistakes we react.

As parents, part of the emotion generated when we watch our children play sports is that we want to spare them pain, embarrassment, and frustration. Some kids can miss the fly ball in the field and shrug it off over ice cream an hour later. Other kids take those moments harder. Age plays a role in how kids react to making mistakes too. Your child may be extremely sensitive now at the age of eight and less sensitive later at age fifteen or vice versa. A lot will depend on other things that are happening for him or her, such as peer influence, other activities, and other stresses, such as school performance.

Don't try to suppress or deny the strong emotions you have when watching your child play sports. Strong emotions, especially when they're not socially acceptable, such as feeling angry toward an official or even your own child, can be unpleasant and so we like to pretend they don't exist. That's a mistake.

Feelings aren't good or bad, it's what we do or don't do with them that counts. You can run out on the field or you can suppress the urge. When parents realize that it's perfectly understandable and normal to get emotional over their child's sports, they are better able to deal with their feelings. When you're aware of and accepting of your emotions, you're less likely to be blindsided and have a reaction you find hard to control, like running out onto the field and making a fool out of yourself.

I, like many sports parents, learned this the hard way.

7. Remind yourself, "My child is not me"

I worked with a young ice skater who was talented but wanted to quit because of the constant pressure her mother put upon her to be the best. Her mother, from various accounts, was arguing with the coach, the judges, and was yelling at her daughter during practice.

When we met, one of the first things the mother told me was that she felt she could have been a professional skater herself if only her parents had pushed her, encouraged her, and had been willing to spend the money.

"I'm not going to let this dream die for Sherry," the mother said. "I'll do whatever it takes!"

This mom, however, assumed that skating was Sherry's dream. Sherry, on the other hand, liked skating, but loved animals. She dreamed of becoming a veterinarian one day, not a professional skater. When the girl said this aloud (apparently not for the first time), her mother didn't listen. She just steamrolled right over her daughter's dream and said, "Well, you can become a vet after you go for the gold."

This mom, clearly on a crusade to make her daughter a skater, whether or not the girl even wanted to skate, is an extreme example of a common problem. Many sports parents assume that their children have the same passions, goals, and dreams that they do. Many parents, and I mean many, mistakenly believe that their children are, if not clones of themselves, then at least very similar. They therefore see their children as opportunities to relive a piece of their own history and get it right. Or they think, "Sherry's just like me so I know she really wants to do this" and "She'll thank me later."

, we have a tendency to project our own wishes,
eams onto our children. It's perfectly understand-
: want our kids to feel cheated or left out when it
ts, especially if that's how we felt. That's natural.
I know that desire comes from the heart. But remember, when it
comes to sports parenting—it's not your intention that matters.
It's your actions.

When you find yourself pushing your child hard or are disappointed by what they want to do, take a step back and
remind yourself, "My child is not a mini version of me."
Respect the fact that your child has her own dreams and goals.
Your child is a separate person. Nurture and encourage her
toward her dreams and goals, even if that means giving up a
dream of your own.

8. Ask yourself, "Why do I care so much if my child wins?"

A few years ago, at one of my son's hockey games, a player on his team failed to score during a tied game. Because of his mistake, the other team got control of the puck and scored the winning goal. The boy was wearing Wayne Gretzky's number on his shirt. From the sideline his father shouted, "All the time and money I put into your hockey, you should play like Gretzky." Though the father added a "ha, ha" and though he appeared to be joking, it was obvious to me and many of the other parents that there was a part of this dad that meant it. There was an expectation on the father's part that his son, with all the training, conditioning, camps, and practice, shouldn't be making mistakes, and in fact, should be playing like a superstar and winning.

It's certainly not negative to want your child to win or to be successful in sports or in academics or eventually in business for that matter. It becomes a problem, however, when your definition of success in sports becomes so narrow that it only allows for winning. When we were kids, playing sports, making a good effort, teamwork, and physical fitness were highly valued. Now, what matters most is whether or not your child wins.

Now, not winning equals failure.

With that message, the level of pressure to win often gives youth sports competition a negative, sometimes even life or death, quality. It makes the competitive environment supercharged and very intense. When that happens, sports becomes no fun.

Understanding, or uncovering, the reasons why you want your child to win may not always be easy, but it's worth doing.

It doesn't mean you have a character flaw or you're a bad parent. It simply means that you need to do some soul searching. Your effort now can mean the difference between being an overboard sports parent who embarrasses himself and his child by yelling from the stands or being a supportive one.

If having a winner in sports is important to you, ask yourself this question: *"What payoff do I get when my child wins?"*

When we want something badly for our children, so badly that we behave in ways that aren't helpful for kids, it can mean we're trying to fulfill a need for ourselves. It's normal to feel good when your child wins, it's normal to want him to win, but when you *need* him to win in order to feel good about yourself, you have a problem. For example, do you feel like having a winner proves you're a worthwhile parent? Do you crave the recognition of being the parent with the star athlete? Do you feel like you're not making the same mistakes your parents made with you? Does it mean your daughter will have a sense of pride in her accomplishments that you never had?

If you can answer yes to any of these questions, you may be trying to feel good about yourself through your children's athletic accomplishments. This is a very common problem. Be willing to take an honest look at yourself. No, it's not necessarily fun. We don't like to see ourselves as anything less than the terrific parents we try to be. But the payoff is tremendous. You become a more aware sports parent who can offer true support and encouragement to your child.

9. Make peace with your own sports experience

Moms and dads who go overboard in sports often share painful memories of their own sports experiences, or lack thereof, with me. Jackie, a forty-five-year-old mom of three girls, remembers watching her brothers play football and baseball in the backyard:

My three brothers always played together and I was always left out. I wasn't allowed to play. And it wasn't my brothers who excluded me; it was my mother. I remember once when I asked why I couldn't join the boys she leaned down and said to me, 'What's wrong with you? Girls don't play rough like that.' I know it was a different time back then and girls weren't encouraged to play sports the way they are now, but I can still remember her face when she said it, like she was disgusted with me for asking. I will never let my girls feel that way about wanting to get dirty, be aggressive, or play rough in sports.

Consequently, Jackie has enthusiastically "encouraged" her three daughters to play sports. However, she felt that her twelve-year-old daughter, Hannah, held back too much and didn't take risks in sports, especially in field hockey. "She's too timid," Jackie said, one of her frequent criticisms of Hannah's game. They argued a lot. Hannah told me she just wanted her mom to butt out and let her play.

It was obvious to me (and probably to you too) that Jackie was trying to heal a wound from her past. However, Jackie wasn't connecting the fact that because she wasn't allowed to play sports, to get dirty, to be aggressive, and have the kind of fun she wanted as a child, she was going overboard in parenting her three girls in sports. Eventually Jackie understood that the important thing to her was that her girls be encouraged and supported in sports if they wanted to play and she had gone overboard with that desire because of her own painful past.

Think about your own sports memories. Chances are, these are not random memories. Like Jackie's, they can offer significant clues as to how you feel about yourself or what you experienced as a child. You only remember early experiences if they are significant enough to have made a lasting impact. Many sports parents still carry the memories, the wounds, the scars, the hopes and dreams that playing, or not playing, sports has left upon them from their own childhoods. These unhealed wounds can fuel your behavior as a sports parent. Many of us block out the painful sports memories and try not to think about them at all. Unfortunately, this isn't an effective coping mechanism. We can still be influenced by our early experiences, even if we don't consciously think about them. The feelings of anger, shame, and disappointment these memories generate can easily express themselves in the tone of voice we use to talk about a game, the pressure we put on our kids to perform, or the importance of winning in sports that we communicate to our children.

Parents who thrive when their children win often feel unaccomplished themselves in sports. Do you wish you had been a super athlete? Do you feel like an underachiever in sports?

If you discover that you're trying to heal your own painful sports history through your child's, I encourage you to do the following:

- **Accept how you feel.** Many people try to deny how they feel because they think it's inappropriate or silly. One dad said to me, "I feel ridiculous that it bothers me that I never played sports as a kid. I'm a prize-winning physicist. What does it matter now?" But it does matter. Your pain is your pain. Don't judge the feelings you have, just accept them. When you allow painful feelings to come out in the open you're less likely to be influenced by them in a negative way. It's hard to close your eyes to your feelings and behaviors once they've been opened.

- **Be honest with your child.** I gave Jackie a lot of credit because she was able to tell Hannah, "I was trying not to do to you what my mom did to me, only I went too far. I was pressuring you to play the way I wanted you to play. I'm sorry and I'm going to do better in the future." It's not easy to admit we're wrong, especially to our kids because we feel the pressure to always do right by them. But trust me, your child will most likely appreciate and respect you for being open.

- **Set your own athletic goals.** You may not be able to play a team sport but you can still find out who you are as an athlete. You can challenge yourself and feel accomplished. Join a gym. Many high schools and community colleges offer volleyball and basketball to adults, so sign up. Jackie, Hannah's mom, is now a soccer coach for a girls' recreational team (her daughters don't play on the team). One dad who was putting tremendous pressure on his son to achieve in football, challenged himself to focus less on his son's football career and more on his own athletic activities. Though he no longer wanted to play competitive football, he began training and running races and has set a goal to complete a half marathon within a year. By focusing on his own athletic accomplishments, he was able to not focus so heavily on his son's.

Once you understand and openly acknowledge any unfinished business or painful experience that you still carry from your own sports history that's influencing you as a sports parent, you are on the road to successful sports parenting. With the pressures sports-playing kids face today, they truly need the help and guidance of their parents. But Mom and Dad can't "be there" until they understand what *really* motivates their desire to have a winning athlete.

10. Modify your involvement, if necessary

As a sports parent, your intention is to "help" your child but it's your actions that are helpful or unhelpful. Your son will let you know that your behavior is a problem directly by saying something like, "Dad, when you come to my games you make me nervous" or "I don't like when you yell at me from the stands." Your daughter may be telling you to "back off" through her nonverbal communication, such as hanging her head when you tell her how to improve her serve. You think you're helping and being supportive but your child is letting you know otherwise. If he's telling you that you're creating stress and pressure to win you need to change your behavior. He doesn't want another coach or an overboard sports parent, he wants a mom or dad.

If you're an overboard or overinvolved sports parent I encourage you to take the following three steps to become less involved:

1. **Set limits on your behavior.** If your child doesn't like your standing too close to the sidelines, then you're not allowed to leave the stands, no matter how much you want to go give him a piece of helpful advice. Some parents have to limit the number of practices and games they attend or make the rule of no sports talk once you leave the field. Some overboard sports moms and dads need to have very clear behavioral guidelines set for them. Other parents are able to change simply with awareness, but if you still have a problem, you need to impose limits on your behavior and stick to it. As you

will discover, changing your behavior is a very effective tool in alleviating your child's stress.

2. **Challenge your belief system about what you can and can't do for your child.** If you're thinking, "If I'm at more games, she'll play even better" or "The only way she'll get honest feedback is if I'm there to give it to her," you're wrong! More is not always better when it comes to sports. You cannot transform a child with average athletic talent into a superstar athlete by being in the stands and providing encouragement. Rather, you create stress and pressure for your child.

3. **Give yourself a mantra.** Come up with a short phrase to help snap you back when you're on the verge of losing control, such as "No yelling from the stands," "Coach doesn't need my advice," or "Ethan's needs are more important than mine." When you're sitting at a game and you get the urge to start yelling or to give the coach a piece of advice, repeat this phrase to yourself over and over again. Many parents find that it gives them a positive thought to focus on until the urge to shout or interfere passes.

I have worked with some pretty tough cases in which a mom or dad was going overboard and had a very hard time stopping. If they can correct their behavior I am completely confident that you can too. Think about what's at stake—your child's health, happiness, and ability to enjoy sports. That's a good motivator for most moms and dads.

11. Be a role model for good sportsmanship

Kids learn how to be good sports by watching their parents. Parents who are good sports have kids who are good sports. Here are four guidelines for setting the standard of good sportsmanship behavior:

- **Talk to the parents of the other team.** These people are not your enemies or to be avoided. Be social. Extend yourself in friendship. Your children will see you do this and get the idea that it's okay to be friendly to people they're competing with.

- **Congratulate any player who does a good job— regardless of whether or not she's your child or what team she's on.** Saying, "Good play," "Your team did a great job today," or "Good game," will encourage your child to support and be respectful of other players and their accomplishments.

- **Thank the coaches and the referees for their time.** We often assume they know we're appreciative. Let's tell them.

- **Point out professional athletes in the media who show respect for the rules and those who don't.** Discuss why some players get fines for inappropriate behavior, such as punching another player or spitting on an official, and why it's not acceptable to behave the same way. When watching an NBA playoff game with my sons, one player on the losing team was trying to start a fight with a player on the winning team. To his credit, the player on the winning team walked away. I told my sons, "I'm really impressed that he was able to do that. That must have been hard, but it was the right thing to do."

II

• • • • • • • • • • •

COMPETITION:

It's not good or bad—
it's how your child learns to handle it

Because there is a winner and a loser, sports is by its very nature competitive. And contrary to what we hear and believe, competition is not bad. Competition is not good either. It's simply a by-product of playing sports.

What can be good or bad is how kids experience competition in sports. When kids play with a "winning is the only reason to play sports" or "a win at all costs" attitude, sports competition is usually a negative experience. When kids play with a "do your best" and "give it your all" attitude, sports competition is usually a positive experience.

With parental guidance, participation in competitive youth sports can help kids learn how to handle stressful performance situations. Handling pressure situations is a skill that can benefit your child for the rest of her life in a variety of situations, like academics and the business world. When kids compete in a positive environment at young ages and learn how to manage the difficult emotions and frightening physical sensations that competition creates, like fear, anxiety, and butterflies in the stomach, they are far more likely to continue playing sports as they grow.

When your sports-playing child has the tools to deal with his or her feelings around competition—both physical and emotional—you won't have to protect him from competition becoming a negative experience; he will protect himself.

12. Talk about the benefits of competition

The increasingly competitive nature of youth sports has gotten a lot of negative press lately, especially because there have been several high-profile incidents of violence at youth sports games. Educators, doctors, and concerned parents believe that kids are under too much pressure to win. We hear that the pressure is taking a toll on the health and happiness of young athletes. I read articles in professional and consumer publications about the detrimental health effects of competitive stress in youth sports.

It's true; too many kids are under too much pressure to win. It's not a good thing to be stressed to the point where just the thought of playing soccer makes an eleven-year-old want to vomit. That level of pressure to win shouldn't exist in youth sports. Too much negative competition (i.e., "win at all costs") is not a good thing.

But let's not forget that competition has spurred athletes to do some amazing things, to be their best, and to go the extra mile. You can be sure that superstar athletes like Tiger Woods feel the pressure to perform and win. Perhaps the reason they are successful is that they have learned to manage the pressure and play through it.

It's important for parents and kids to understand that competitive stress—the emotions and physical sensations that can be experienced during the pressure of competition, like fear and sweaty palms—though uncomfortable or unpleasant—is not a bad thing. In fact, competitive stress, when kids know how to manage it (I'll discuss how to do this later in this section) is often a positive motivator. Stress is a natural by-product of performance. Would you tell your child who loves to sing never to get up on a stage and sing if she feels nervous beforehand? Of course not. The same is true for a tennis player or swimmer.

It doesn't matter if your son or daughter plays on the town softball team, the high school field hockey team, or the college lacrosse team, every athlete, no matter how positive the competitive environment, experiences the symptoms of competitive stress. You simply can't protect your child from experiencing competitive stress in competitive sports, nor should you try. Because kids perform when they play sports they will always experience some level of competitive stress. Sports is about performance. When anyone performs, whether it's on the football field, a stage, or in a classroom, she will feel some degree of nervousness, whether that translates as the pregame sweaty palms or an all-out anxiety attack, with troubled breathing and dizziness. The key is making sure your child plays in a positive competitive environment (where the adults or her peers are not putting too much pressure on her to perform and win) *and* giving your child the tools (discussed later in this section) to cope with the unpleasant and uncomfortable feelings that competition fosters.

You should also:

- **Discuss negative competition versus positive competition.** Kids need to know how you draw the line on what's acceptable in competition and what's not. Use examples from your child's sporting life whenever possible. I told my daughter Talia: "Remember when Mr. Jacobs yelled at Sandra for losing the ball? Well, your mom and I don't agree with how he handled that. We think that's not a good way to behave during competition. We think it would have been better if Mr. Jacobs had said, 'Good try,' to Sandra because she was trying hard. But we don't control what other adults do."

- **Remind your child that competition has many benefits.** Let her know that competition can help her to focus, concentrate, and challenge herself to perform better. You don't have to make it a big, serious discussion. You can slip your ideas into the conversation when it's appropriate. When my son Eli was talking about an amazing play he had seen during a basketball game on television, I made the comment, "You know, that's one of the things I love about playing against other people. It really gives you the chance to see what you can do." He just said, "Yeah," and walked away, but over time, he will get the message that one of the benefits of sports competition is to push yourself to see what you can accomplish.

13. Give your child permission to be nervous

Tiger Woods said in an interview that he's always nervous when he's playing golf. Kids need to know that even professional players who look calm on the outside get butterflies in their stomachs before and during competition. Children lack the experience to know that most people get nervous before they have to perform. That's why Mom and Dad need to provide the bigger picture. You can do this by taking the following steps:

- **Explain that pregame jitters are totally normal.** Letting kids know that anticipatory anxiety is a normal response to a performance situation eases their stress and tension. Kids worry that they are somehow different or not as good as the other kids. Feeling nervous, stressed out, or panicky can be frightening feelings for kids. Those feelings often provide the proof that they are in fact different or not as good as their peers. When they don't know how to manage their stressful feelings, the stress can build to a point where their ability to perform is impaired. Muscles tighten or concentration is shattered by disturbing thoughts, such as "If I screw this up, everyone will think I'm stupid" or "I can't do this," and suddenly they can't perform. Your child needs to understand that the challenge of all athletes is to work through the fear, nervousness, and anxiety, and trust that when the game starts, "I'll be fine." Let your boy or girl know that many athletes find that those uncomfortable sensations of competitive stress, like dry mouth, shaking legs, and sweating palms, can actually enhance performance and help them go that extra mile.

- **Personalize the experience.** Use examples from your own experience, whether they're sports-related or not, to soothe your child's fears. You can say, "I don't play soccer, but I had to get up in front of a whole room full of people once and tell them about a project I'm working on. I was so nervous. My mouth got dry and my palms were sweating. But I took a few deep breaths, reminded myself that I was prepared, and guess what? As soon as I started talking, I felt better. I got through it and so will you." Personalizing the experience will show that you really do understand what he's feeling and give him hope that he can get through it too.

- **Reassure him that he *can* deal with it.** When you have a positive attitude about competitive stress your child will come to have one too. Let him know that you will help him find a way to deal with it—no matter how long it takes. Once kids understand that those wobbling legs, headaches, dread, and dry mouths are common to all athletes they feel normal. Your empathy and reassurance show her that there are ways of handling her uncomfortable feelings.

- **Describe "competitive stress" as "competitive excitement" instead.** We experience many of the same physical sensations when we're excited as when we're nervous, like shallow breathing, pounding hearts, and shaky legs. Thinking of those symptoms as "excitement" rather than "stress" helps put a positive spin on the experience.

14. Watch for the warning signs of competitive stress

Your son or daughter may be able to tell you, "Mom, I feel like I'm going to throw up when I'm at bat," but many kids, especially kids under the age of twelve, will often need help naming what they're feeling and understanding why they feel it. Some kids won't tell you they need help if they think you might be upset with them. As one eleven-year-old put it, "I hate telling my dad stuff when I think he's going to yell at me or tell me to act like a man. I'm just a kid."

That's why moms and dads need to be on the lookout for the signs and symptoms of competitive stress. Kids who need help dealing with competitive stress in sports will often express themselves through their nonverbal communication. Here are some of the most common ways that kids will let you know they need help managing their feelings and emotions generated by sports competition:

- **Physical Issues.** A healthy child will suddenly tell you he or she is sick when it's time to go to practice or a game. Before, during, or after a game or practice, your child complains of headaches, dizziness, stomach upset, hot flashes, and other sudden physical complaints.

- **Performance Difficulties.** A child who plays consistently well in practice but who plays poorly during a game or competition may be experiencing competitive stress.

- **Personality Changes.** A child who is normally even-tempered throws a bat during practice if he or she strikes out. The calm child strikes another teammate or an opponent during a game. The outgoing child withdraws or the shy child curses when participating in sports activities.

- **Behavioral Changes.** You notice that your child is suddenly eating less, eating more than usual, or having trouble falling asleep. A change in your child's usual behavior patterns is a sign that she's suffering from competitive stress. Some behavioral changes occur on the field and some occur off the field.

- **Emotional Upset.** Your child shows signs of nervousness, anxiety, anger, or sadness, especially when on the way to practice, during a game, or after playing the sport. Your child dwells on mistakes or blows them out of proportion.

If you notice any of the above warning signs, don't panic. All sports-playing kids will occasionally have a tantrum, cry, or get an upset stomach before a big game. Remember, pressure is built into performance. You can't change that about sports. The feelings that competition creates can be uncomfortable, but they are unavoidable and to be expected. Some kids handle the stress of competition better than others. A lot of it has to do with your child's athletic ability, self-esteem, and confidence levels at the time.

If your child exhibits unusual or troubling behavior now and then, or once or twice, even if it's unsettling, I wouldn't worry too much about it. Kids have phases of behavior that they cycle in and out of. It's the pattern of frequent and/or persistent behavior that you need to address.

Though not an absolute rule, "frequent" or "persistent" means that the behavior occurs around four or five times within a short period of time, whether it's a thrown bat at four games in a row or crying in the car on the way home after five lost games. That's a pattern. The pattern lets you know that your child is most likely stressed out and needs to learn how to manage her stress.

15. Encourage positive thinking

Young athletes who are not handling competitive stress in a positive way often think in black-and-white terms. They think, "If I miss this ball, I stink" or "If I don't make this shot, I'll be letting Coach down." This kind of negative thinking creates an enormous amount of stress and pressure around sports performance. Worst of all, it can lead to a self-fulfilling prophecy. If you tell yourself something over and over again, eventually it will become the reality. So the child who thinks, "I know I'm going to fall off this balance beam" or "I always fall off this balance beam" is more likely to fall off the beam than one who thinks, "I've practiced hard and I know I can do it."

It's important for moms and dads to encourage positive thinking in young athletes, especially when they're experiencing competitive stress in a negative, unhelpful way. Positive thoughts will help counter the stress and empower your child to work through any unpleasant feelings he or she experiences. Here are three effective ways you can do this:

- **Give your child a positive mantra to recite when she gets nervous.** Kids often need their parents to give them the positive words or phrases to tell themselves, otherwise they come up with a negative statement. Keep it simple, like "I am a winner" or "I can do this." Devi was a fourteen-year-old field hockey player whose parents taught her to tell herself, "I just need to give it my best and I'll be fine" over and over again so she could take the pressure off herself. They instructed her to push any other thoughts out of her mind and keep repeating, "I just need to give it my best and I'll be fine." Over time, these kinds of positive thoughts become automatic and can replace the negative and unhelpful ones.

- **Teach your child to talk back to negative thoughts.** Don't just tell your child not to think negative thoughts, tell him he needs to answer them with positive thoughts. Instead of ignoring a negative thought like, "I just know I'm going to miss," your child needs to talk back to it by saying, "I don't know I'm going to miss. I've practiced very hard. I made this shot in practice yesterday." One swimmer I worked with kept a rubber band around his wrist. Whenever he thought a negative thought about his swimming, like "the boys on the other team look so much stronger than I do," he had to snap it. Then he would tell himself something positive like, "They might be bigger but I'm lighter and faster so I have a good chance of winning." When you have to answer your thoughts, it forces you to become more aware of them. It then becomes harder for negative thoughts, like "I'm not as good as they are," to slip in and do their dirty work like create anxiety, fear, and tension.

- **Encourage your child to talk to himself the same way he encourages and talks to his teammates.** You will often hear kids tell one another supportive and positive statements like, "Shake it off" or "You'll get it next time." Let your child know that he needs to talk to himself in the same supportive way. Again, this is about creating awareness in your child. He will start to notice that he is naturally very encouraging and supportive of his teammates and that he can extend the same encouragement and support to himself.

It can take time to change the way a child thinks. But if we are consistent in reminding kids that positive thoughts can create a positive outcome, it will work. Sports-playing kids who think positive thoughts feel more confident and are also more able to keep a good attitude when they make mistakes or lose.

16. Practice breathing and relaxation with your child

When we're nervous or excited, we tend to take shallow breaths. This creates even more nervousness or anxiety because we feel like we can't breathe. This is not a pleasant feeling for anyone and it's especially distressing for young athletes who don't understand why they feel panicky. Kids need to be taught how to breathe to relieve stress.

Practice breathing at home first. Sit together facing each other. Tell your child to close his eyes. Narrate the process: "Breathe in through your nose to a count of four. Breathe deeply. Push your stomach out. Let your entire chest fill with air. Then hold that breath for a count of four. Then exhale slowly to a count of eight. Imagine exhaling your stress and tension out of your body. This is how you can breathe before or during the game when you get nervous. Remember when you're getting ready for your turn or you're feeling nervous, breathe like this a few times and you will feel better."

Many moms and dads will give their children signals during games or matches to remind them to breathe. One dad of a wrestler points to his chest and then raises himself out of his seat as if he's being filled with air. This reminds his son to breathe because when he's nervous, he forgets to breathe deeply.

Deep breathing is a simple activity but the results are amazing. Sports-playing kids can instantly feel less stressed out and empowered to handle their feelings just by taking a few good, deep breaths. But like most adults, we are not conditioned to breathe properly and beneficially when we're nervous. Kids don't usually figure this out their own. They need to be shown how to breathe in order to feel calmer.

17. Model calmness for your child

You are the model for your child in all things, including the ability to handle stress and pressure. Whether or not you realize it, you profoundly influence your child's attitudes about the meaning of winning, of competition, of making mistakes. When Courtney saw her dad "freaking out" or yelling because an official made a bad call against her, she told me: "I would see people looking at me and I thought I was going to pass out."

When their parents get upset and overwhelmed, kids tend to get upset, overwhelmed, and even more nervous than they were in the first place. If your son is nervous and he sees you wringing your hands and pacing the sidelines, do you think that is going to help him become less nervous? Of course not. Just the opposite will happen.

You help your child learn how to calm down by providing the example of being calm. If you're stressed out or upset in front of your child you have an opportunity to show him that being upset is okay but calming down is important. You then show him how you're calming yourself. When you talk to a child who is stressed out, speak slowly and softly. Keep your gestures to a minimum.

Remind your child how to "slow down" when he gets his physical signals that his anxiety and/or stress is hitting. Speak and move slowly and calmly as you explain, "When your hands start to sweat or you breathe hard or get dizzy this means you're feeling nervous and that's okay. You need to take a 'time out.' This means you stop and take a deep breath because when we're nervous we forget to take deep breaths."

When your daughter sees you acting calmly in a stressful

situation she'll learn, "The best way to handle it is to calm down." Your son will see you taking deep breaths and he'll remember, "That makes me feel better." Moms and dads have a tremendous influence in helping their kids learn how to handle stress by setting a positive example.

18. Teach your child to recognize his yellow warning light

Fifteen-year-old Tyrell wanted to quit the basketball team because, he said, "I can't take the heat anymore." His parents and his coach felt that with his level of ability he had a good shot at winning an academic scholarship. They wanted him to keep playing but his stress level had escalated to the point where he had fainted on the court.

One of the first things I did to help Tyrell manage his stress was help him find what I call his "yellow warning light." I explained that rarely do you feel fine one moment and then find yourself on the floor the next. There's usually a buildup to negative competitive stress and it begins either with physical sensations and/or disturbing or worrisome thoughts. Here is how I helped Tyrell discover his yellow lights during competition:

"When you start to get nervous on the court, what do you feel like? What do you think about?" I asked.

"I'm not thinking anything except about the game," he said.

"Okay," I said. "So what are you thinking about the game? Are you thinking about winning? About the other team? About your coach?"

"About how I hope we win. About how I hope I don't screw up."

"How would you screw up?"

"By dropping the ball."

"What do you feel physically when you first start worrying that you'll drop the ball?" I asked.

"My palms start to sweat and I hate that."

"Why do you hate it?" I asked.

"I don't know." He shrugged. "I guess I think I'm getting nervous."

"What do you worry about when you're nervous?" I asked.

"I guess that if my palms keep sweating I'm going to drop the ball."

"And what happens if you drop the ball?"

"Everyone will be disappointed in me," he said. "Maybe I won't get the scholarship everyone keeps talking about."

For Tyrell, the thought, "What if I drop the ball?" was his yellow light. This was the thought that triggered his sweating palms. The more his palms sweated, the surer he was that he would drop the ball. By the time he was thinking about losing a shot at the scholarship he had already gone crashing through the red light. The time for Tyrell to catch himself was when he first started to think thoughts like, "I hope I don't drop the ball" and when his palms began to sweat.

I let Tyrell know that his sweating palms were his body's way of letting him know he was getting nervous and needed help managing his feelings of fear, which were totally normal. I worked with him to develop strategies he could use to calm down and counter his negative thoughts, like giving himself positive messages and taking deep breaths, while the light was still yellow.

For Katie, a perfectly healthy track runner, her yellow light started with a physical sensation. "I feel fine but then I get this achy, weird feeling in my leg," she told me. "Like my leg is getting tired before the rest of me is." The tired feeling in her muscle then led her to think, "What if something is wrong with my leg and I can't finish. If I can't finish I can't go to the state finals . . ." The thought that something was wrong with her leg caused her breathing to get heavier and she couldn't run as fast.

Kids will often tell you what triggers their feelings if you know to ask. Probe for information by asking questions like, "Before you dropped the ball, how did you feel?" "When it was your turn at bat, what thoughts were going through your mind?"

If your child shrugs and says, "I don't know," which many kids will answer because they really don't know, prompt them for additional information. Put words in their mouths if you have to. This is okay to do, especially for kids ten and under who don't yet know how to articulate their feelings. Do this by asking, "When the ball comes to you do you feel your hands sweat/knees shake/mouth go dry/dizzy?"

Once you isolate the physical part, work on the mental. Try to discover what thoughts they're thinking that led to or resulted from feeling worried, anxious, and/or stressed. Simply ask, "What were you thinking when the ball came to you?" Again, it's okay to put some words into their mouths, especially for younger children. "Were you thinking, 'Everyone will be disappointed if I miss?' or 'I'm no good at this'?"

Don't worry so much about figuring out which came first, the thought or the physical feeling. Just help your child understand how they work off one another to create the stressful feelings and the fear that send him crashing into that red-light zone.

By teaching your child to tune into her body and mind, you can teach her how to deal with her feelings while she's still in the yellow-light warning zone. When she knows how to calm herself and to challenge negative thoughts she will be empowered to manage her stress before it's full-blown or feels too frightening.

19. Rework negative competitive attitudes into positive ones

Jason is in the fourth grade. He's a soccer hound. All he wants to do is play against other kids in games and tournaments. He gets so excited when he wins. He runs in circles and jumps and whoops. It's like he glows for hours afterward. When he loses he takes it hard. He won't look you in the eye and he can't eat. He puts so much pressure on himself to win. What can we do?

We hear so much about parents and coaches pressuring kids to win that we forget that there are many young athletes who apply the pressure themselves. Kids are natural competitors. Ask any third grader, "Who is the fastest runner in the class?" I can practically guarantee that the child will know the answer. When you put a group of kids on a field they will want to show themselves and others what they're made of. And this isn't a bad thing. It's nature taking its course.

For kids, sports is a place where they can figure out who they are in the world. It's where they can begin to figure out, What am I good at? What are my skills? What can I do? One of the most accessible ways they can do this is by comparing themselves to other kids. Athletic skill contributes significantly to identity. Being one of the best players helps them get noticed and helps them feel confident and accepted—no small thing for both the eight-year-old and the sixteen-year-old trying to figure out who he or she is in the world.

But sometimes kids feel too much pressure to fit in or they worry that they can only fit in if they are athletically talented and so winning in sports takes on greater importance. Some children are, by nature, perfectionists and will therefore take losing hard. These are the kids who are hard on themselves across the board, whether it's hockey, the math test, or arts and crafts.

If you're worried that your child is too focused on winning or is putting too much pressure on himself to win, one important way to help balance his attitude comes from helping him understand the many purposes of competition. Kids need to be told by parents and coaches that winning is not the only goal of competition. It's not the most important reason to play sports. All sports-playing kids need to hear this important message on a regular basis—weekly or before games at least. But kids who are by nature perfectionists or are internally driven to compete—that is, they put the pressure to win on themselves, especially need to hear that winning isn't everything on a more intensive level. Talk to them every day about teamwork, about self-sacrifice, about being a part of a larger team community. When your child wins, you certainly want to show that you are proud, but try to notice other accomplishments your child made during the game as well. Jason's parents will now tell him, "You played great and we saw how you helped that boy who fell down. We're really proud of you for that." When he loses they empathize with him about his loss but they remind him, "You win some and you lose some, and that's okay."

When parents are consistent in reminding kids of the many good reasons to play sports, slowly but surely, even super competitors will catch on. More often than not, winning and losing start to become secondary. When a parent says, "You don't have to win the game to be a winner to us," and really means it, kids know and are profoundly influenced by this positive, healthy message.

You *can* rework negative competitive attitudes into positive ones. I've seen it happen many times in a variety of situations. But this transformation rarely happens on its own. Kids need parents to give them perspective about sports; that sports has many dimensions, not just winning and losing.

20. Talk to your child's coach, if necessary

You've taught your child how to breathe correctly. You encourage positive thinking. You send him positive messages that winning isn't everything. But your boy just isn't able to manage his stress or he's just not enjoying himself. It may be that your child's coach is putting your child under too much pressure to win and creating a negative competitive environment. The best way to find out is to talk to your child about his experience. Ask him open-ended questions that require more than a yes or no answer, like: "How are you getting along with Coach this season?" or "You don't seem to be enjoying hockey as much this year. What's changed?"

You should attend some practices and games and pay attention to how the coach treats the kids. Does he yell? Does he reward for effort or just results? Does he give positive feedback? If you work full time and have trouble getting to the games, you can speak with other parents who have children on your child's team and get their opinions. If you find that your child's coach is pressuring him in a way that's not good for him, you should speak up on his behalf. You can't expect a child, especially a child under the age of seventeen, to be able to set limits or to advocate for herself with an authority figure—a person who has power over your child because of his or her position.

I do encourage you to allow your child to be present during the conversation. This is how your child will learn to self-advocate in the future with coaches and other authority figures. Keep it simple. Don't apologize or make excuses. Let the coach know what he or she is specifically doing that is causing the stress and creating the negative competitive environment. Be specific about how you would like that behavior to change. Be honest and direct but always use polite language. Here are two examples of what real-life parents have said to their child's coaches:

> *Alison doesn't like the way you correct her in front of the other kids. Can you take her aside and give her feedback?*

and

> *We feel that Malcolm is being pushed too hard to score points. Can you emphasize teamwork and effort more than winning?*

Leave it open for the coach to give his or her viewpoint or to agree or disagree. The coach may say, "Well, I correct all the kids in front of each other, that's how they learn." Or "I don't push Malcolm any harder than I push anyone else."

What can you do then?

Stick to your original request. You need to find out if the coach is willing to work with you. Be firm, but again, be polite.

> *I understand that you do that with all the girls but being corrected in front of all the other kids doesn't work for Alison. It makes her nervous. Can you take her aside? Is that something you can do?*

or

> *That may well be true, but Malcolm is not having a good experience because he's being pushed too hard. I*

need to know if you can encourage him to work hard and be a good teammate rather than win the game.

Most coaches are good people, working hard to bring out the best in our kids. They don't set out to create stress and pressure in your child's life, though sometimes this happens. Talk to the coach. You may be able to work out a solution.

I know many parents who don't care 100 percent for a coach's values about winning or who don't necessarily like the coach's style all of the time. Many of these parents are able to help their kids deal with the stress in spite of this. Think of it as an opportunity to help your child deal with authority figures or difficult personalities. You can encourage your child to take what's helpful from the coach and leave the rest behind. You can remind kids that it's possible to not like everything about a person but still be able to work with someone and get along with that individual.

One dad encouraged his daughter to focus, not on her coach's criticisms, but on her teammates' compliments and positive feedback. This helped her to feel less pressure and more supported.

(For additional information on dealing with your child's coach, including making the decision to pull your child from a team, see Coaching Concerns, chapter 5.)

21. Recognize your own competitive nature

Knowing how competitive you are in all areas of your life and not just in sports can help you better parent your child in sports.

Natalie was a talented sixteen-year-old tennis player who suddenly wanted to quit the game she had always loved so much. Normally fun-loving and outgoing, Natalie had become sullen and withdrawn. She was not playing to her true ability. Her parents were worried that any opportunity she might have at a scholarship was in jeopardy.

When I asked her parents about their own competitive natures, Mrs. Martino announced, "Oh, I'm not competitive at all. He's the one," she said, pointing at her husband. "He gets all wound up about Natalie's tennis, not me. You should see him when he loses at golf."

Mrs. Martino saw herself as the noncompetitive one and her husband as the driven competitive one. Mr. Martino agreed with this assessment. "Yes, I am competitive," he admitted somewhat sheepishly. However, further discussion revealed that Mrs. Martino was quite competitive when it came to winning other kinds of competitions, whether in fund-raising for the Junior League or the church's pie baking contest. As it turned out, both parents were influencing their daughter's attitude that "I have to win," not just the parent who was obviously competitive about sports.

Like the Martinos, it's quite common for moms and dads to have black-and-white ideas about their competitive natures. Many people see themselves as either supercompetitive or not competitive at all. And it's common for them to hold a judgment about it, like being noncompetitive is favorable to being competitive or vice versa. People tell me, "I'm competitive, but not *too* competitive," as if being competitive is a bad thing.

Here are two things you need to know about taking your competitive inventory:

ONE: BEING COMPETITIVE ISN'T GOOD OR BAD; IT'S HOW WE REACT TO WINNING AND LOSING THAT CAN BE POSITIVE OR NEGATIVE

Believing that being competitive is somehow bad or incorrect is an impediment for seeing yourself as you really are. Remember, it's how we play the game and how we handle winning or losing that influences our kids the most.

TWO: MOST PEOPLE ARE NOT EQUALLY COMPETITIVE IN ALL AREAS OF THEIR LIVES

I've asked hundreds of moms and dads to rate themselves (you can too) on a scale of one to ten, with one being noncompetitive and ten being the most competitive, in the following five most common competitive situations: sports and games, work, social status, family and friends, and competitive with yourself. It is rare that a person has ever given me the same number for each competitive situation.

What people often discover is that they are usually not entirely competitive or entirely noncompetitive. You're not competitive about sports but competitive when it comes to your career. You're not competitive when it comes to your career but competitive about your lawn and garden. You're not competitive in general, but when you play Trivial Pursuit with your family, you want to dominate the game. Your children observe your competitive attitudes and they are affected by them.

My older brother Neal and I are still competitive with each other when it comes to sports and even games like Scrabble.

During one of our Scrabble tournaments we teased each other and got excited when we scored over the other. Neal would say, "See, I'm still the smarter big brother," and I'd say, "Not for long. You are going down if we have to play all day!"

I used to think that it didn't matter if we competed fiercely with one another as long as we got along after the game, which we always have. Then I saw my sons playing basketball in the same competitive way. Eli was tormenting Ari by holding the ball over his head out of Ari's reach. Eli was saying, "I'm older, so I'm better." When Ari managed to get the ball back, he threw it at Eli's head and said, "You might be older, but I'll prove you're not better."

I realized that through my behavior with my own brother, I was encouraging my sons to be competitive with one another in their sports play. I realized that I needed to monitor my competitive behavior when Neal and I play Scrabble or any other game when my children are present.

Taking your competitive inventory is not about getting you to admit that you're extremely competitive or not competitive at all. It's not about judging yourself. It's about understanding when you want to win in different areas of your life so you can be aware of how you're influencing your child's attitudes about winning and losing. Your children learn their competitive attitudes by watching you. As I learned firsthand, children often mimic their parents' behavior, even when the parents don't want them to.

22. Avoid the competitive parenting trap

Some parents want their kids to win at sports because they are competitive with other parents. Keeping up with the Joneses now includes the Joneses' children's sports accomplishments. More sports parents than ever are having the kind of conversation I heard at my son's soccer game:

> "Did I tell you, Brandon was recruited for the travel soccer team even though he's only eleven years old?" said one mom.
>
> "Oh, that's so nice," said the other mom. "We wish our William had the time to play soccer but the Little League coach said he just couldn't face the season without him. And he did get accepted to that camp . . ."

On it goes . . .

Parents spend a lot of time together when their kids play on the same team, especially with year-round play and travel teams. Among parents there is a sometimes subtle, and sometimes not-so-subtle, tendency to compare their children's skill levels and accomplishments. On the surface, people say, "Teamwork is the important thing" or "I'm just happy that my Johnny gives it his all," but underneath the surface, the emotions are brewing. We're all just human. So yes, Mom and Dad would love to see Johnny score the game-winning point.

It is unspoken but all parents know: There is a certain status and prestige that the parents of the star athletes of the team have in the eyes of the other parents. Suppose you have an athletically talented child. That means you are the mom or dad who people pay special attention to at practices and games. People say things like, "Oh, you're Alex's mom and dad," in such a way that communicates that "Hey, you're the mom and dad of that incredibly talented boy Alex."

Of course, it's wonderful to feel pride in your child's accomplishments. The problem occurs when you use or need that status or prestige of your child's performance to fulfill a need in yourself—perhaps the need to feel successful or to be admired. The problem occurs when you are dependent upon your child's performance to give you that feeling. When parents fall into the competitive sports parenting trap, they want, often not consciously, the status, prestige, and bragging rights that come from having an athletically talented child. These parents turn up the pressure on the child to win and bring home the medals and the trophies.

One of the most helpful things you can do to get out of, or avoid ever falling into, the competitive parenting trap is to avoid other competitive parents. Kathleen, a sports mom, told me why she avoids competitive parents:

> When you're with people who are always comparing their children's times, it's hard not to do it too. And it's hard not to start expecting your child to be as good as these other parents' kids. I started wanting Jenna to swim fast just to show those parents up. I was getting stressed out at her meets. My husband said all I talked about was how fast Jenna swam over this or that other kid. He didn't like this and I didn't like this part of myself, either. I had become so competitive . . .
>
> Now, I make it a point to be friendly to everyone, but I only sit with the more laid-back moms and dads. We don't talk about times all the time. Every conversation is not a comparison. We even talk about movies and restaurants.

What a nice change from the other parents I used to sit with. I don't get stressed out about Jenna's times anymore. If she's fast, great, if not, there's next time.

Yes, it's normal to be proud of your child's accomplishments, but don't get into the habit of bragging about your child or comparing your child's accomplishments when talking with other sports parents. This can lead you to become competitive with other parents. Make a point to expose yourself and your child to other parents who have the same healthy and balanced attitude that winning isn't the only reason to play sports.

low your child to switch to
ess-competitive or non-
npetitive sport

I truly believe that there is a sport that every child can feel competent in and enjoy playing. Parents need to understand that it doesn't have to be competitive to count. Not all kids are suited to the so-called traditional competitive team sports like baseball, football, and basketball. Some kids just don't enjoy competitive team sports. Some kids simply aren't at the age or don't have the emotional maturity to handle the spotlight pressure of sports like softball, gymnastics, and tennis. These kids do better in sports like soccer where if you make a mistake (unless you're the goalie) you're not going to be under a bright light with all eyes staring just at you.

Aiden, a seventeen-year-old boy who was first in his class academically, told me, "Dr. Fish, I work so hard in school, I don't want to work so hard getting a base hit. I'm just no good at it." His parents were worried that without a team sport he wouldn't get accepted into an Ivy League college.

I asked Aiden's parents what good it would be if Aiden got into Harvard but was burnt out by the time he was eighteen from having so much pressure in his life? They agreed not to pressure him to play baseball anymore but encouraged him to ride his bicycle on a regular basis.

Like Aiden's parents, you may need to widen your view of the sports world. Not all sports are team sports. Not all sports have to be competitive to count. You can even just let your child take the season off from sports and just play. There's no law that says a child must play an organized or team sport at least once a year. Parents are concerned that their child will somehow fall behind in athletics or will be at a disadvantage in sports or in the college application process. This just isn't true. I personally know many kids who took a break from the stress of competitive sports and then bloomed later in the same sport. I've worked with kids who either switched to less competitive sports or have taken a complete break from all organized sports. These kids are all wonderfully healthy, active, and happy. As far as I know, most of them have gone off to college and are doing very well.

But if you feel strongly that your boy or girl needs to participate in some kind of sport, cycling, rock climbing, canoeing, running, and hiking are all excellent, challenging, and fun sports that can give kids the opportunity to compete against themselves rather than other people. While participating in these sports, kids can gain confidence, meet personal goals, and develop athletic skills. Noncompetitive sports play can be an important step in preparing a child for competition at a later time.

In a year or so if you think your child is ready to handle a competitive sport try it again. If it's still not working, give it more time. If your child isn't physically and/or emotionally ready to deal with the pressure of competitive sports this year, it's nothing to worry about. A lot can change with kids within a few months or a year. Continue to encourage your child in spontaneous play and less competitive sports. Most of all, believe that your child is fine and will not grow up at a disadvantage. After a break, many kids want to return to sports or discover sports that they feel more comfortable with.

24. Consider the age factor

I have seen kids who appear to handle stress and pressure well at the age of seven or eight, but then they move up along the competitive sports chain as they age and the stakes get higher, the competition gets tougher, and suddenly they're stressed out. There's nothing wrong when this happens. It simply means your child is in a different place now with competitive stress than he was a year ago. He needs to adjust to a new competitive environment. He will have to fine tune the skills he was using before to deal with competition to suit his new situation. So don't overreact, just give him some time.

You may have two children close in age who play sports. One may not be bothered by competitive stress and one may have a difficult time handling it. I've heard parents say things like, "But I don't understand why it's so easy for Molly to go out there and play but her sister Grace practically has to be carried onto the field."

Both children are perfectly normal. Kids do not all start out with the same ability to handle competitive stress. They're all different in this regard, even siblings. It's important to respect individual differences in a child's temperament and ability to handle stress and not draw comparisons to a child's sibling or teammates. At my daughter's soccer game I heard a mom ask her daughter, "Why are you always so nervous? Can't you be more like Talia? Look at her. She's having a great time."

While I'm sure her mom was just trying to help, the message to this girl was not "I'm trying to help you." It was "You're not okay because you're nervous." It's hurtful to children when we treat what is only normal kid behavior like a problem or something to hide. Parents are proud of their children when they seem unfazed by the stress of competition. They believe they will grow up with an advantage that will help them succeed in college and beyond. This can happen, but you need to be aware that all kids will cycle in and out of phases where they seem fine under pressure and at other times, they will need more help and support. The calm six-year-old T-ball player becomes the nervous ten-year-old soccer player. The nervous ten-year-old becomes the confident fourteen-year-old athlete . . .

Many kids who have trouble dealing with competitive stress at young ages can learn to handle the pressure better with age, usually starting around twelve and thirteen years old. Kids around this age have more experience handling competition whether it be in sports, academics, or other competitive situations. This experience helps. Older kids know better that they can "handle" themselves in pressure situations because they've done it in the past. They are more readily able to adopt behavioral or cognitive skills to help themselves, like positive thinking or relaxation techniques.

However, once kids reach the age of twelve or so, peer pressure starts to matter more, which can contribute to making a child feel more pressure. Peer pressure can also cause a child who always handled pressure well to suddenly fear the spotlight. When the pressure to fit in and perform well in the eyes of one's peers takes on importance, a child who has never felt competitive stress can experience problems.

Both your child and the competitive environment she plays in will change constantly. There's just no predicting for certain how a child will start out or end up handling competitive stress. The most important thing for sports parents to remember is that all young athletes can learn, no matter what their starting point or age, to handle competitive stress and pressure better; sometimes they just a need a break from competitive sports in order to do this.

You have the most significant role in helping your child learn to manage the many feelings that will be generated by sports competition. As she ages, give her the tools and resources to deal with competition and she will be fine, even when the competitive environment turns negative. Most of all, believe in your child's ability to learn how to deal with the many emotions and physical sensations brought on by sports competition.

PerPormance:

Practice doesn't always make perfect

Parents often ask, "How can I get my child to play to the top of her game?" Some performance issues can be solved by making simple technical adjustments while others are rooted in emotion or fear. Fortunately, there are many proactive steps parents can take to help their young athletes play to the best of their abilities.

25. Make sure that your child is technically able to perform her sport

If your child can't perform well in his sport, he may have a technical issue. It's fairly common that children, especially ages twelve and under, don't perform well in sports because they don't have all the technical skills they need. For example, is your son's throwing motion proper? Is your daughter holding her bat or hockey stick correctly? These technical issues do cause performance problems. A few years ago, a girl on my daughter's soccer team didn't understand all the rules and parameters of play, so of course she made mistakes. Not having the right technical skills, including understanding all the rules, can cause your child to make mistakes, feel embarrassed, and lose confidence.

Here are four guidelines for assessing and dealing with a technical issue affecting performance:

- **Know that kids won't always ask you for help.** Your nine-year-old won't tell you, "Dad, I don't think I'm kicking the soccer ball correctly," because he doesn't know that he's doing it incorrectly. Older kids, especially twelve and up, are reluctant to ask for help out of embarrassment. They think, "I should know how to play better" or "I should be able to figure this out on my own." Moms and dads shouldn't assume that their child will always know or is willing to ask for help if she needs it.

- **Observe your child's technique while playing.** How does her technique and performance compare to the other kids on the team? She may be athletically immature but you may discover that this is the norm, especially for kids under the age of nine or ten, who are playing an organized sport for the first time. If you're not sure if she's playing correctly, ask the coach or another parent for input.

- **Don't assume that your child will get all the help he needs from his coach.** Many sports parents mistakenly think that because their child is playing on a team that he must be getting all the help he needs in developing his skills. Remember, not all coaches are created equally; some are better at giving direction and instruction than others. Many players under the age of ten are coached by volunteer parents who don't always realize that a child is having a technical problem and needs additional help. Many performance problems, once pointed out, can be easily solved by some one-on-one coaching and/or additional practice.

- **Determine if your child has a physical issue.** A boy on my son's baseball team became a dramatically better player once he started wearing glasses. Again, you can't always rely on a child to tell you, "I can see close up but I can't see far away" or "My knee hurts all the time," so parents need to be on the lookout. Kids don't always know when a physical issue is causing the technical problem. Even ill-fitting shoes can cause performance problems for athletes. When trying to assess the source of a performance issue, ask your child probing questions like, "Can you see clearly? Is the sun bothering your eyes? Can you hear the coach call the plays? Does any part of your body hurt you? Do your shoes feel too tight or too big?" Often you will discover that behind the performance issues lies a physical problem.

26. Prepare your child for not making the team

With more kids playing sports, it's harder now to get a position on the junior high and high school teams. Some of the recreational teams like the all-stars or the elite travel teams are even harder to make. Your child may be technically good at his sport, but he still might get cut. The competition for spots on these teams can be fierce. Not only do parents have to help their kids cope with the competitive stress of being on a team, they have to help them cope with the stress and pressure of making the team in the first place.

A friend of my son was crushed when he didn't make the school baseball team. He lost his appetite. He didn't want to play catch with his dad or his friends. When his parents asked me to talk with him, Robert blurted out: "I feel like the biggest loser in the whole world!"

Kids take not making the team hard. So do their parents. Robert's parents were stunned that he didn't make it. "But he's such a good player," they told me and I agreed. I had seen Robert play. He was good. But there were other better players trying out for his position. It happens.

It also happens that a deserving child doesn't make the team for reasons that have nothing to do with her performance. Though this wasn't the case with Robert, I meet parents who tell me how the all-star team in their community or the high school football coach seems to play favorites or gives favors. The coach knows a girl's father from work and that girl gets a position on the team even though another girl is a better player. This is a growing problem (for more advice on handling an unfair coach, see Coaching Concerns, chapter 5).

If your child is trying out for the team, you need to prepare him for the possibility that he won't make it. Here are some guidelines to follow:

DON'T:

- **Discourage.** For example, you don't want to say, "Well, you're probably not going to make it because there are so many other kids who are better." Don't be negative, be realistic.

- **Go overboard with encouragement.** You also don't want to go too far the other way and say, "We're winners in our family! We go for it and get it!" or "Winners never quit and quitters never win . . ." This is not preparing a child for the possibility of not making it. This kind of overboard cheerleading puts more pressure on kids. They think, "Oh no, if I don't make it, Dad will think I'm a quitter."

- **Make your child into a victim.** In an attempt to make kids feel better some parents say things like, "You've been robbed! That coach had something against you." Or "They were out to get you." This only heaps another dimension of emotion and stress upon your child.

- **Deny her feelings of loss.** If you say, "Who wants to be on that stupid field hockey team anyway," you're only diminishing what was important to her. You're denying her feelings and that only makes things worse. Instead, acknowledge her loss by saying, "I know you're very disappointed. It's really hard to get cut like that."

DO:

- **Give a positive reality check.** You want to prepare kids for the possibility of not making the team without discouraging them from trying. Focus on effort and not outcome. You can say something like: "I can see how hard you're working to improve your game. I know you really want a place on the team. But there are over thirty-five freshmen who are trying out for field hockey this year. Only six of you will make it. I'm not trying to discourage you. I just want you to know that the competition is very stiff. It can happen that we work really hard and still don't get something. It makes us feel bad for a while, but the important thing is to try. If we don't try our best we never know."

- **Give her positive options.** Your daughter will feel less pressure about trying out for the team if she knows it's not the end of the world if she doesn't make it. Let her know: "I want you to remember that if for some reason, you don't make it this year, you can still try out next year. I'll work with you every Saturday. There's also a girls hockey team forming at the new sports arena over in the shopping center. We can check that out." If she doesn't make the team, remind her that she does have options to play other sports.

27. Maintain realistic expectations about clutch performance

I watched as Julie, an eleven-year-old ice skater, landed her first jump of the competition on an obviously unsteady leg. Next to me, her mother sighed loudly, as if to say, "Here we go again."

As Julie's final jump approached, her shoulders were hunched forward and when I saw her face, my heart truly went out to her. She looked absolutely terrified. She was supposed to perform a double rotation in the air but she only rotated once before falling. Her mother turned to me and said, "See, she did it—again. She always loses it in the clutch."

More and more, parents and coaches believe that in the heat of the competitive moment, a true athlete should be able to rise to the occasion and do whatever it takes to win, especially during the win or lose—or what is commonly called a "clutch"—moment in sports.

For a figure skater like Julie, a clutch moment is when she does her jumps in competition. For a tennis player, it could be making the backhand shots when the score is tied. For a soccer goalie, it's making the big saves when it counts. For a football player, it's kicking a last second field goal. In ordinary situations, such as practices or routine games, these clutch moments pose no problem or obstacle to the athlete. It's when the pressure gets turned up during a play-off game, a tryout in front of a college recruiter, or because a parent is watching that the athlete cannot perform to his or her usual standard. It is commonly called "choking" during a clutch or key-game moment.

Clutch performance is a lot to ask for from any athlete, let alone an eleven-year-old girl! Yet many parents and coaches do expect kids, even as young as six or seven, to pull it out "in the clutch." As youth sports continues to get more focused on winning, many unrealistic performance demands are heaped upon youngsters. Young people are told, whether verbally or nonverbally, that they have been coached and conditioned and now it's time to show what they're made of. The performance demands heaped upon kids who specialize in a sport can be even more demanding. The belief is that a child who receives a great deal of coaching and intensive training should be able to perform, no matter what.

The professional athletes who perform flawlessly, the ones who can always pull it out "in the clutch" are indeed grown professionals and they are actually quite rare. Even the most celebrated professional athletes occasionally make mistakes and blow it when the heat of competition is turned up high.

Parents need to be reminded that sports can be physically *and* emotionally demanding for kids. When a mom or dad says to me, "I don't understand why Charlie can't perform 'in the clutch,' " I often find that the parent has never played a competitive sport and/or has never played in the high-pressure environment that their children now play in. Sports parents tend to focus on the physical and they forget, or simply don't understand, how much of sports is actually mental.

Young athletes should not be expected to always, or even consistently, "pull it out in the clutch." Clutch performance is too much to ask for from a young athlete who is developing her skills—both physical and mental—and growing into her body. Kids need the emotional space in sports to learn how to deal with competitive pressure over time, to make mistakes, and to have fun. Let your child know that it's okay to make mistakes, even if the game is on the line. Reassure her that she's learning how to deal with the stress of competition and that there's nothing wrong with her.

The children of moms and dads who keep their performance expectations realistic often are better able to enjoy sports and not get burned out early on from too much pressure.

28. Avoid labeling your child a "choker"

Never tell a child, "You choked" or "You always lose it in the clutch." And avoid generalizations like, "Sammy always gets nervous when he plays sports." Without realizing it, we can set kids up to live up to these narrow definitions of who they are and what they are capable of accomplishing. It can be quite emotionally damaging to communicate to a child that he has an Achilles' heel or some kind of inherent weakness when it comes to sports and handling those big pressure-filled moments. Your child can end up believing it and living up to the label of "choker." He or she may think, "When the going gets tough, I can't deal with it, so why even try?"

Some kids see how upset their parents are when they can't perform and come to their own conclusions. They think, "Look at how upset Mom is. She is really worried that something is wrong with me. This is really a big problem. There is something wrong with me. I'm a choker."

Labeling a child, no matter what her age, as a choker can have devastating consequences that can reach well beyond the child's athletic career. But with kids who are twelve and up, we need to be especially careful not to label performance issues as personality traits. At this age, it's easier for a child's self-image issues to go beyond sports and affect other areas of their lives. Teenagers are trying so hard to fit in and their identities are in constant flux and therefore less stable. They are more susceptible at this time to believing negative things about themselves. I worked with a seventeen-year-old diver who told me, "Dr. Fish, you're wasting your time on me. Ever since I was twelve I've been a choker. I messed up on the

SATs for the same reason. I just can't hack the pressure. It's hopeless."

What a self-defeating attitude for a young person to have! Kids can come to believe that they just can't handle pressure or they're just no good in intense situations. This is certainly not the attitude parents want to convey to their children, yet time and time again this happens, simply because parents make generalizations about their child's athletic ability or panic when there's a clutch-performance issue.

Just because a child does sometimes miss in those clutch moments, it doesn't mean he or she will *never* be able to handle the stress of competition. Even if your child has developed an issue around clutch performance, it's no cause for alarm.

Choking is *not* a mysterious element of a flawed personality or character. It's a form of competitive stress. And just like a child who gets nervous in the car on the way to a game or a child who can't sleep before a big match, a child who can't perform during key moments can learn how to deal with the stress that's causing his muscles to freeze or her timing to be thrown off.

There is an erroneous belief in our culture that some of us are born able to handle pressure and others of us are doomed to become chokers. Let me assure you, no child is born a choker and no athlete is a choker by nature. These fears are simply groundless.

When parents think of and communicate "choking" as a "performance challenge" or "clutch performance issue" instead, it can help their young athletes have a positive and proactive attitude. Removing the negative label that the word "choker" carries can significantly help a young athlete deal with and overcome a clutch performance issue, before it spills over into other areas of her life.

29. Ask your child's coach to avoid labels and generalizations

Your child's coach may mean well by saying, "Billy, you choked," but coaches have a great deal of influence over kids, especially when they're under the age of twelve. Kids seek the approval of their coach. Just as it can devastate kids to be labeled a choker by their parents, coaches too can harm children with labels or by making generalizations about a child's performance.

If your child's coach is saying things like, "Sophie just isn't a strong outfielder," "Max always loses it in the clutch," or "If you choke again, we'll probably lose," I advise you speak with the coach. Be nice, polite, and firm. Here are a few options for what you might say:

> *We are trying to help Max deal with his "performance issue" and we prefer to use that term rather than "choking." Can you do that?*

> *I understand that "choking" is a common term used in sports but it upsets Sophie to be called a "choker." We find she's been much more receptive when we talk about her "challenge with her backhand." Can you use that term too?*

> *You probably don't realize that Dora doesn't like to be told that she "choked." What can we say to give her feedback if she misses the foul shot again?*

Coaches, like parents, almost always have good intentions when it comes to helping kids overcome performance issues. However, what they say and how they say it can have a tremendous influence upon young athletes.

30. Help your child name his or her fear

Because young athletes lack experience and perspective, the fear of failure in sports can seem huge and can take on a life or death quality. Kids think, "No one will like me if I miss," "I should just give up," or "I can't do anything right." The mental anxiety connected to the fear of failure makes young athletes freeze up or try too hard. When you try too hard your body naturally reacts with tension. In sports, tension paralyzes your muscles and cripples your repetitive memory, which enable us to perform on autopilot in pressure situations. An athlete's natural ability to perform is hampered—your son will stand there and strike out and your daughter will not be able to rotate on a jump, even when you know he or she can do better.

Young athletes with performance issues are often told by parents, coaches, and teammates, "Don't think about striking out" or "Tune out those negative thoughts, just ignore them." I don't find this "ignore it and it will go away" approach helpful. This is avoidance thinking, not positive thinking. One of the first things you need to do to help an athlete deal with a performance challenge is help him name his fear. By naming what we fear, we take away its power. Naming what we fear allows us to successfully counter it with positive thinking, relaxation techniques, and the other strategies I discuss in the last section, to help the athlete calm down so his natural abilities can flow.

Get your child talking about what she is afraid of if she makes a mistake or if he misses the ball.

Some parents will come to me when they've already gotten to this point. They'll tell me:

We keep telling Tyrell he won't drop the ball. We remind him that he almost never has dropped the ball. We got him to name his fear, but it hasn't helped.

Or

Tracy obsesses about striking out. I tell her it's okay to strike out, that major league hitters strike out but I'm not getting through.

The problem often persists because "dropping the ball" or "striking out" is not the emotional part of the fear. I tell moms and dads, take it to the next "what if" level. Find out exactly why dropping the ball, striking out, falling, or missing the jump would be so scary or why it's so high stakes. Keep asking "what if" questions until you uncover the emotional fear. Here's how Tracy's mom helped her ten-year-old daughter name her emotional fear:

MOM: *Okay, let's say you do strike out? What would happen?*
TRACY: *I won't get on base.*
MOM: *And what if you don't get on base?*
TRACY: *Don't you get it? Coach will be really mad at me, especially if that's the last out.*
MOM: *I've seen Coach when another girl strikes out or makes a mistake. He doesn't seem to get mad. He doesn't yell or anything like that.*
TRACY: *Well . . . I know he gets disappointed.*
MOM: *You don't like to disappoint him.*
TRACY: *No.*
MOM: *And what if you disappointed him? Would he say, "You let me down" or "You're not as good as I thought you were?"*

TRACY: No. *He just gets quiet and writes on his clipboard.*
MOM: *Coach is always writing on his clipboard.*
TRACY: *Yeah. But what if he's writing, "Tracy stinks."*
MOM: *What if he wrote that? What would happen?*
TRACY: *Maybe some other people would read it and then everyone would think I stink.*

For Tracy, the thought of disappointing her coach and having people think she wasn't good at softball were crippling her natural talents. Once Tracy's mom understood Tracy's fear was not striking out, but being perceived as a failure by her coach and teammates, she was able to help Tracy. She worked with her on deep breathing (see point 15) and visualization techniques (see pp. 83–85) and provided daily reminders to her daughter that "everyone makes mistakes." Once he understood the issue, Tracy's coach was supportive too. If she made a mistake or struck out, he would make it a point to verbally reassure her, saying, "Don't worry about it, Tracy" or "Shake it off. You'll get it next time," and not to write on his clipboard. As her stress and anxiety diminished, Tracy's game improved and she was able to play to her natural abilities and enjoy the rest of the season.

31. Teach your child how to visualize successful performance

If your son is challenged at those high-stake moments, or if he's just trying to become a better overall performer, one of the most helpful things you can do is teach him how to visualize successful performance. Visualizing builds confidence and empowers kids to feel more in control. With mental practice, the high-stress situation or the routine at-bat moment become familiar and kids have experience dealing with it. In fact, studies have shown that athletes who practice *and* visualize perform better than athletes who simply practice.

Denise is a high school track coach who had gone to college on a partial athletic scholarship and learned visualization techniques in high school. "I don't think I would have been as successful as I was in college, winning the state championship in 1992, if my dad hadn't taught me how to visualize myself sailing over the finish line. I teach it to my girls. It works!"

Children over the age of eight can usually be taught how to visualize. Visualization focuses on the senses, paying attention to what you see, smell, hear, and feel in order to create a real-seeming event out of one's imagination. Begin with a simple nonathletic exercise, like exercise #1 below, to build her visualization skills.

EXERCISE #1: Have your child sit in a comfortable and quiet place with her eyes closed. After a few deep breaths tell her to imagine that she's eating an orange. Ask her to describe how it feels in her hand and how it smells. What does the orange look like; is it big or small? Is it perfectly orange or does it have some green patches? Is it hard or soft? Then prompt her to take her time and imagine peeling it. Ask her if there are seeds. Get her to describe the taste. Do this exercise every day for a week or two. Start with five minutes and then work her up to about ten minutes. Vary the fruit or have her visualize herself eating her favorite food, sitting on the beach, or taking a ride on a roller coaster. The point is to stimulate your child's imagination using her senses.

EXERCISE #2: When your child has practiced visualization in other situations for a few weeks, move on to an athletic situation. Have her sit in a comfortable and quiet place with her eyes closed. After she takes a few deep breaths, ask her to describe the temperature, what she's wearing, the playing field, and what her teammates are doing. Guide her through normal performance situations first and then into the high-stress athletic situation. If she is a tennis player for example, you would encourage her to see herself successfully making her serve. Then ask her to describe how it feels to make a perfect serve. What does her form look like? Does she feel proud of herself? What words does she say to herself, like "I knew I could do it"? What does she do next? Do this exercise once or twice a day for about ten minutes or so. If she's having trouble visualizing, continue to encourage her. Most kids catch on within a few weeks of practice.

You can also guide your child to imagine that she has just missed or made a mistake. Help her to visualize herself successfully recovering. What words would she use—i.e., "That's okay, I'll get the next one" or "Shake it off"? Guide her in seeing herself take a few deep breaths. This exercise can keep young athletes from panicking when something unexpected happens or when they make a mistake.

EXERCISE #3: Encourage your child to create a "snapshot" image of herself after she's made the successful serve or after the match is over and she's won. Ask her: What does her expression look like? What is she doing with her body, i.e., jumping up and down or raising her arms in victory? What are you thinking as this "picture" was taken? A snapshot image is a "picture" of herself she can learn to instantly call to mind while she's on the field.

EXERCISE #4: Guide your child in pretending that she's starring in a "movie" of her tennis match or other sport. Begin by having her imagine that she's in a movie theater, sitting in a comfortable seat. Ask her what she sees and feels in the movie. If she tells you something negative, like "I feel like I'm going to miss again," gently guide her into seeing and feeling something positive instead.

Teaching kids visualization techniques helps them learn to take responsibility for their thoughts. It builds confidence and is a useful skill they can use in other areas of their lives, like taking the SATs, doing well on a college or job interview, or trying out for the school play.

52. Encourage peak performance but avoid creating pressure

"Peak performance" occurs when an athlete plays to the utmost of his or her abilities during a high-stakes game or pressure-filled competitive situation. When an athlete is "in the zone" everything comes together—practice, skills, attitude, and confidence—and he or she can do no wrong. These are the golden moments in sports for athletes, when your son scores the game-winning goal or your daughter makes the foul shot during the playoff.

As parents, it's exciting and rewarding to see your child playing at his peak or knowing that she's in the zone. Parents often ask me, "How can I encourage Ellie to play at her peak?" or "What can I do to help Jason get 'in the zone'?" There is no magic formula to follow to ensure peak performance. You can send your child to camp and to clinics in the off-season and yet he may still play to an average level. Some kids do benefit from extra coaching and practice, but oftentimes, it's just good timing, when everything seems to come together and work in your child's favor, such as: natural ability, skill development, good coaching, and love of the sport. Sometimes just plain luck allows children to play at their peak. But there are two steps you can take to encourage your child to play at his or her peak:

- **Point out what your child is doing well or how she's improved.** During competitive play, your child may not be aware that she's playing to her peak. Or she may know she's "in the zone," but she can't tell you why or how she got there. Try to help her figure it out. Let her know what she did differently, "You were holding your racket a little higher and that seemed to give you better control" or "Those deep breathing exercises seemed to help you relax." Knowing what they are doing well can help kids to tune into their own performance or see the benefits of their stress management techniques. Knowing how she got "in the zone" can help her get there again or to stay there a little longer the next time.

- **Give balanced feedback.** Let your child know what she's doing well and where she needs improvement. Both are important for kids to know. Knowing what they're doing well gives kids positive reinforcement. Positive reinforcement builds self-esteem and confidence. When they have good self-esteem and self-confidence levels, kids are more open to hearing about where they need work. They are not threatened or worried when learning their mistakes or weak performance areas. But remember, you're a parent, not a coach, so don't go overboard in providing feedback.

33. Accept that practice doesn't always make perfect

When it comes to improving your child's performance through extra practice, understand that in youth sports *more isn't always better.* In certain situations, additional practice can help kids improve their technical skills and gain confidence as athletes. I've seen kids with specific technical problems, like kids who weren't holding a racket correctly or throwing a football properly, improve and thrive with extra practice. But some parents go overboard. When a parent pushes a child to not only attend her regularly scheduled practices but also to practice more after dinner, on the weekends, or in the off-season, it can lead to burnout.

Kids go overboard with practice too. Kiley was a high school freshman who wanted to make one of Boston's elite crew teams. "I would see the boats on the river and I would think it was so cool," she told me. She was told by the coach that to get a tryout she needed to have more upper body strength. Kiley started lifting every day. She worked out on her dad's rowing machine every night. But in the end, Kiley just didn't have the upper body strength to row competitively. The weight lifting exhausted her. She wasn't built for it. Her parents had to intervene and stop her from practicing. They did the best thing they could, they helped Kiley find a sport she was good at and more physically suited to. Kiley is now a senior and runs track on her university's team.

Here are three important factors to consider before encouraging, or allowing, your child to practice more:

- **Interest level.** Johnny's dad was sure Johnny would start to love golf if only he played it enough. He was wrong. The boy disliked the game even more. You can't force a child to love a sport by making him practice. If you have to drag your child to practice or force him to shoot baskets with you in the driveway, that's a good sign that your child isn't interested in the sport as much as you are. On the other hand, a child who seeks out additional play or practice on her own can benefit from the extra work. But the bottom line is clear: You can't force a child to be interested and enthusiastic in a sport if she's not.

- **Energy level.** Though we often think that kids have limitless amounts of energy, they don't. Kids get tired too. Kids today have busy lives. They have schoolwork and numerous activities and hobbies to keep up with. One dad I know encouraged his fourteen-year-old son to put in extra weight training time to improve his football performance. He built the boy a mini gym in their basement to make the workouts easier for him to fit into the mornings and the weekends. Rather than get stronger, the boy became exhausted and couldn't finish the season. This dad wanted to know what was wrong with his son. There was nothing wrong with his son except that he was lifting too many weights. He was too young to be maintaining such an intensive conditioning program, especially unsupervised. Parents need to be certain a child is physically capable of handling additional practice and conditioning, especially when they are ten and under and their bodies are not yet as strong as they will one day become.

- **Natural Aptitude.** Though it can be tough for kids and parents to accept, practice cannot take the place of natural ability. You cannot pitch a ball at ninety miles an hour unless you were born with the right kind of arm strength, aim, and balance. You can practice and practice in your backyard for hours every day, but you can't change nature. The important thing to remember is that every child has some athletic aptitude. There is a sport out there that she can be good at and enjoy. If a child is faced with relentless performance problems despite a lot of practice, what fun is she having? Parents need to intervene and steer kids to a better choice in sports. They need to send the message: "You're not a failure because you've tried to play hockey. You have to try new things to find out what works and doesn't work for you."

IV

. . . .

SPECIALIZATION:

More isn't necessarily better

Twenty years ago, the norm for young athletes was to play a sport in its traditional season, like soccer or football in the fall, and then move on to the next sport as the season changed, like basketball or wrestling in the winter.

Today, a child can play just about any sport he or she wants year-round. There are fall baseball leagues, summer basketball leagues, indoor golf ranges and tennis courts, indoor and outdoor soccer fields and hockey rinks. Just about the only sport that remains a one-season sport is football, but even that's starting to change as more youth football leagues are instituting spring practice. And then of course, there are the summer camps and clinics built around a single sport.

But parents are asking: Is it good for my child to specialize in one sport?

34. Try to wait until your child is at least fourteen or fifteen years old before specializing

Kids under the age of fourteen should be encouraged to play a wide variety of sports year-round. When your child reaches high school age, around fourteen or fifteen years old, he or she will be in a better position to specialize in a sport. At this age, there are three factors that make specialization an appropriate step:

- **Physically, she will be more mature.** At the beginning of high school, most kids begin to equalize in growth rates. Your child won't be ahead athletically simply because he was an early bloomer. And this works the other way too. Late bloomers can now get in the game. You may have had a child who was not very good at soccer at age nine who suddenly at the age of fifteen is very good at the game.

  A child must be physically prepared to meet the demands of extended practices and conditioning. Most kids are simply not prepared until they are older.

  The other physical advantage of not specializing before high school age is that your child will have had the opportunity to develop a wide range of motor and athletic skills from having played a variety of sports. She will not get this benefit if she plays only one sport.

- **Emotionally, he will be mature enough to better handle the demands of specialized sports play.** The stress of competition and dealing with different coaches can be a challenge. By the time kids are in high school, they are better able to apply past experience to present situations and can learn from mistakes. Your son is less likely to see himself as Paul the ice hockey player. Instead, he can see himself as Paul, a boy who is good at, and likes, ice hockey. Older kids are also in a better position to understand what it means to make a commitment of time and energy to a particular sport.

- **Interest level can be more accurately gauged.** A child who can't get enough of peewee football or tennis at the age of eight may simply lose interest by the time he or she finishes middle school. Kids don't always know what they like and don't like until they're doing it and this is totally normal. Young athletes can benefit greatly from playing a variety of sports so they can discover what they like.

Before you give your child permission to specialize, make sure that all three of these important components—the physical, emotional, and interest level—are in place. Your child might hit them at a slightly younger age or he may not get there until he's sixteen years old. Don't rush. I've seen kids who were physically prepared to play a sport before they were emotionally ready; it usually backfires if you let them specialize anyway.

Thomas was six foot five when he was fifteen. He loved the game of basketball and was very good at it. Physically, he was clearly ready to specialize in basketball. His interest level was there as well. However, emotionally Thomas still had some maturing to do. He had great difficulty dealing with his teammates, who resented his abilities. He did not know how to be a gracious winner or loser. He ended up stressed out and upset a good deal of the time because his teammates didn't like him. His parents pulled him off the team and gave him another year to get emotionally ready to compete. It worked. When Thomas played the following year his coach remarked that he was like a different person. He was able to deal with his teammates and handle winning and losing much more successfully.

35. . . . Or proceed with caution

You genuinely believe that your child is gifted and is destined for athletic greatness. You have a child in the minority, one of the few who thrives and blooms when specializing in one sport when she's ten years old. The problem is, you are not the most objective person when it comes to making this decision.

We all want to think that our son is a natural at golf or our daughter is a gifted swimmer. It's natural for parents to see their children's potential and they want to help them run with it. One dad told me that he was sure his son was going to be good in baseball because baseball "ran" in his family. Athletic ability can certainly run in families but just like eye color and height it can also skip generations and vary widely between siblings.

Even if your child was born with special athletic gifts, pressuring her to play one sport year-round may backfire. She could sustain an overuse injury or burnout and you'll never know what she could have achieved in the sport. If you truly believe your child is gifted in a particular sport and her interest and desire are truly there, and if you want her to specialize before she reaches high school, follow these three guidelines:

- **Have no expectation of greatness, just fun.** Even if your child seems naturally gifted in a sport, recognize that she may be an early bloomer. Her passion and enthusiasm may change over time. Go into it thinking and believing, "I just want my daughter to have fun. That's the most important thing to me." This is not necessarily going to be easy. I've met many parents who say they just want their child to have fun but they only say it because it's the correct thing to say. Their actions and the way they yell at officials or critique their child show me that they want their child to win. Just keep reminding yourself that, "If Becky doesn't enjoy herself, she'll probably stop playing."

- **Take it very, very slowly.** Make sure that your child gets an appropriate amount of rest from her sport by alternating seasons or taking seasons off.

- **See a doctor regularly.** Take your child to a doctor who specializes in pediatric sports medicine. Children can appear healthy, while their bones, joints, and muscles are taking a beating. You absolutely need to get medical feedback if your child is specializing.

36. Be aware of the physical and psychological impact of specialized play

Just because kids are young and have lots of energy doesn't make them immune to overuse injuries and just plain physical wear and tear. In a formal statement the American Pediatric Association (2000) came out against sports specialization for young children because of the stress, overtraining, and burnout associated with playing one sport intensively. Both the Youth Sport Institute and the American College of Sports Medicine recommend avoiding early specialization in sports for the same reasons.

While I don't think you can paint every single child with one brush, I agree that the majority of children playing sports today are physically better off not specializing until the early teen years. Repetitive and overuse injuries are on the rise from specialized sports play and can lead to serious medical conditions. Your doctor or a sports medicine professional can tell you why and in which particular ways your own child may be physically at risk.

But even if your child seems fine and gets a clean bill of health from his doctor, be aware that psychologically, kids who specialize in a sport and play year-round, may derive too much of their identity from being a soccer player, the hockey goalie, the gymnast, or the pitcher. This identification places enormous pressure on sports performance. It's hard for kids to take a break or walk away from a sport, even when it's in their best interest to do so, if their emotional investment is so high.

When the majority of a child's energy is devoted to "being" a particular kind of athlete, it leaves little room for developing and nurturing other interests. If these kids leave the sport, or when it's time to move on to another team, like high school or college and they don't make the cut, many will face a serious identity crisis. I've met kids who don't know who they are if they're not "Judy the tennis player" or "Max the goalie." They don't know who they are and where they fit in.

When kids who heavily identify themselves as a particular kind of athlete leave their sport, they often don't know what to do with themselves. They also feel deeply shamed at having let themselves, their parents, and their coaches down. I have worked with many kids who have become depressed, anxious, rebellious, and troubled as a result of overidentification with a sport.

When a child has no other interests or hobbies, parents should strongly consider putting the brakes on their child's specialized sports participation, at least temporarily. Help your child see that while hockey or tennis is great and fun, there are other great and fun things in life too. Encourage him to try new activities, both sports and nonsports related. Chances are that he'll benefit from this help far more than he will any additional sports training.

37. Don't specialize for the wrong reasons

The experts agree, parents should delay sports specialization until a child's teenage years. However, it's often the parents who refuse to believe in the benefits of waiting to specialize. In today's supercompetitive youth sports culture, it takes courage and faith to be the parent who stands back and says, "I want my child to play a variety of sports" or "Two seasons of organized sports is plenty," when so many families in your community are doing the opposite.

Why don't more parents wait? There are three common reasons, all of them the wrong ones, why so many parents want their children to specialize.

- **Fear that your child will be at a disadvantage.** After a conference, one mom told me that she had taken a stand on nonspecialization for her two sons and has taken a lot of flack for it. Another mom had told her, "I hope your boys will still be able to make the high school team. They'll have some pretty stiff competition."

  "Do you think I'm making a mistake?" she asked me. "Am I hurting my boys' chances to get on the team later?"

  I told her that although I didn't know her boys personally, I have found that most young athletes do benefit from playing a variety of sports and not specializing at young ages. Furthermore, a lot of the young boys who are getting all the intensive training will burn out by the time high school tryouts arrive. And even if her boys didn't make the high school team, there are so many indoor and recreational leagues most kids can usually find a team to play with.

Fear is simply not a good reason to allow or encourage your child to specialize in sports.

- **Guilt that you are cheating your child out of a golden athletic opportunity.** Many parents "confess" to me that they feel guilty about denying their child the opportunity to specialize in a particular sport at a young age. They worry that they're somehow cheating the child or that they're selfish for not wanting to devote so much of the family's time and energy to sports. These sports parents have many valid reasons for making this decision, whether it's a time consideration, fairness to other siblings, or a financial matter, and yet, they feel guilty.

It's hard not to feel like you're cheating your child when so many parents around you are getting on the bus every weekend to follow the travel team. The myth that more is better is so prevalent in youth sports today that you may feel like you're not giving your child a fair shot in athletics if you don't provide more. But trust me, you're not cheating your child.

I ask these moms and dads, "Overall, does your child seem happy and well adjusted?" When they tell me yes, as so many of them do, I tell them the facts about burnout—that it's on the rise and occurs most often with young athletes who specialize before high school age.

When parents tell me that a child is unhappy because he can't specialize, I remind them that the ideal age to specialize is around fourteen or fifteen. "Tell your child you'll revisit the issue then," I advise. "You'll either find your child has lost interest or that he continues to show a passion and enthusiasm. You'll be in a better position to make the decision."

One dad told me, "I think it's ridiculous to schedule our free time around our child's sports activities. Matt plays two seasons a year and that's enough." Many parents agree, but are reluctant to follow. These are the parents who believe the myth that they owe their child the opportunity to get really good at a sport.

Like fear, guilt is an unfounded reason upon which to make a decision as a sports parent.

- **The parents want the status and prestige of the star athlete.** These are the parents who tell themselves, and anyone who will listen, that eight-year-old Paul doesn't want to do anything other than play golf—so we're getting him a personal coach.

 In order to be a successful sports parent, you need to be clear on the reasons why you're encouraging your child to specialize in a sport when just about every expert will tell you that it's better for him to wait until he's older. What are you getting out of it? Are you getting attention or admiration? What need or desire in yourself is fulfilled by your child's athletic career? You have to be very clear about your motives. If you're struggling with this issue, I encourage you to review points 8 to 10 in chapter 1, Awareness.

Make sure your child's interest level and enthusiasm for the sport equal your own. If not, then it's likely that you are pushing your child inappropriately or having her specialize to meet your own goals and not hers.

38. Understand the odds of getting a scholarship are slim

Some parents push their kids to specialize early because they think it will increase the chance of winning an athletic scholarship.

As the dad of three kids who will likely go to college, I can appreciate why parents want their kids to win athletic scholarships. College is expensive. Parents worry, "How am I going to pay for it?" Some parents can send their kids to college only if they get financial aid in the form of an athletic scholarship. An athletic scholarship *can* be a ticket to a college education for an athletically gifted child.

But the odds of winning athletic scholarships, even if your child is a talented athlete, are not good. Only an estimated 1 to 2 percent of all the millions of kids who play sports will actually win an athletic scholarship. There are simply few spots available at colleges and universities that grant athletic scholarships, and the competition is brutal. Even talented—sometimes very talented—athletes get passed over in favor of other, more talented athletes. It happens and it's often devastating for the athlete and her parents.

Stephanie was a track runner who set records at her high school and came in second place at the state finals. She was also an honor roll student. Her parents and coach were sure she was a shoo-in to receive a full scholarship from a large university. Though the passage of Title IX, a 1972 federal law that mandated equal opportunity and funding for girls in sports, has made more athletic scholarships available for girls, one out of three girls now play sports, so more girls are competing for these scholarships. Though Stephanie was good, other girls were even better.

In the end, Stephanie did get a partial scholarship to a college, but it was a letdown. She was looking forward to running track for a big, high-profile school. She wanted to compete at the highest level possible. Her self-esteem took a big blow. It shook her confidence and she had a difficult first year at college.

Stephanie's well-meaning parents made a mistake a lot of sports parents make. They assumed that because Stephanie was a record breaker, she would get a full athletic scholarship. It never occurred to them that she wouldn't get it. They didn't mentally prepare themselves or Stephanie for the possibility. Parents of talented athletes pursuing athletic scholarships need to have a Plan B, just in case. You need to discuss the alternate plan with your child to mentally prepare her. You can say, "We're hoping that you'll get a scholarship. Coach thinks your chances are very good but we have to remind ourselves that there are only a handful of track scholarships given out and a lot of talented girls trying to get them. That's why you're applying to these other schools, just in case . . ."

When kids are pressured to win athletic scholarships and they don't, they often feel guilty that they've let their parents down. You can certainly hope that your child can win money for college, but it shouldn't be the only reason why your child is playing a sport, nor should it be the most important one. It should be a goal tempered with a healthy dose of reality. Tell your child, "It would be great if you get it, but it's okay if you don't. Millions of kids play sports and only a small number get scholarships."

When parents set scholarships up as the main motivation for playing and specializing in a sport, kids do not have fun. They become stressed out and sports becomes an activity they dread.

39. Tell yourself, "More is not always better for children"

Specialization in youth sports has become popular because we believe that more is better. We believe that more playing time, more practice, more coaching, and more conditioning will all lead to a child who is better at a particular sport. How could it not?

We celebrate the superstars like Tiger Woods, who began playing golf at the age of three, and gold medalist figure skater Sarah Hughes, who started skating when she was three too, and we mistakenly believe that in order for a child to become a great athlete, he or she must start training early. We believe that a child who plays a sport in its regular season, such as soccer in the fall, but also plays on an indoor league through the winter and/or spring, will perform a lot better than a child who only plays the regular season. It *seems* logical. If you play three months, you'll be good. If you play eight months, you'll be even better.

Unfortunately, that is usually not the reality.

Most often, a superior athlete is *not* the outcome of specialized sports play. There is no convincing evidence to date to show that early sports specialization improves a child's chances at overall long-term success in the sport. In fact, the emerging trend appears to be the opposite: Kids are dropping out of specialized sports play because they're getting too much practice, too much training, and too much coaching at a young age and they can't sustain this level of intensity into their teen years.

It's important to keep the following in mind:

- **Most of today's elite athletes did not specialize during their developmental years.** Most of the professional athletes I work with began to specialize in their sports when they were in high school and had already participated in a variety of sports.

- **Early interest and aptitude are not reasons to specialize.** Be careful about developing early hopes and expectations about your child's athletic abilities based on his or her early performance. Kids develop at different rates. There are early bloomers and there are late bloomers. What can look like early athletic talent is likely to be average talent by the time your child hits puberty, around twelve for girls and thirteen for boys, and the other kids have caught up. During the early teen years, short boys grow tall almost overnight. Slow kids get fast. Uncoordinated kids get balance and agility. Suddenly, your child has a lot of competition in the sport he or she used to dominate. It can be devastating for a child who has been conditioned by his parents and coaches to believe that he has above-average athletic talent, to discover that now that he's older, he's only as good or not even as good as some of the other kids. This happens all the time to kids who specialize early. The more a child derives identity from athletic ability, the harder the fall will be when she discovers that she now has to work hard, even struggle, to keep up with the other kids.

- **Your child will have fewer options to play other sports later.** Kids who devote all of their energy to one sport miss out on the opportunity to develop their skills in a range of sports. At thirteen, if they stop specializing, they're less prepared to play another sport. They don't even know what other sport they might be good at or enjoy.

- **Exposure to a variety of sports enables your child to develop a wider range of important motor skills.** From gymnastics and skating for example, a child will learn balance and flexibility. From baseball and tennis, children learn eye-hand coordination. But if your child is focusing exclusively on one of these sports, he misses the opportunity to develop other skills during his formative years. It's harder to acquire these skills later on when he's a teenager.

- **Most kids love variety and trying new things.** Specialization increases the chances that your child will become bored. It's quite common that once a child hits thirteen or fourteen, a time of great physical and emotional change, she will find that her passion for ice skating or his great love of hockey has diminished dramatically. Kids who express an early love for a sport often grow out of it, which is perfectly normal kid behavior. These kids often feel guilty too. They know that Mom and Dad have invested a lot of time, energy, and money into developing their sports skills. They feel they've let their parents down.

- **Kids have better socialization skills when they play multiple sports.** When your child plays one sport, he usually plays with the same kids and for the same coaches over and over again. Kids who play multiple sports meet and socialize with more kids and coaches with a range of different personalities and interests.

Many sports parents are surprised, and some are even distressed by the discovery that more practice and more play doesn't guarantee a superior athlete. "You mean I can't create another Michael Jordan out of my son?" one sports dad joked after a talk I had given on the subject. But many sports parents aren't kidding. They really have fallen for the myth that more is good and the earlier the better.

For maybe one third of all kids who do specialize, extra playing time and more training—not necessarily through year-round organized play—can be beneficial. Matt, for example, is a twelve-year-old basketball player on his school's team. Last year, he played the regular season and attended a two-week summer basketball camp from 8 A.M. to 4 P.M. In his free time, he sometimes plays basketball with boys his age at the local YMCA or the playground near his house. These are unstructured pickup games. His parents agreed to send him to the summer camp because Matt wanted to work on his shooting skills and because his two best buddies were also attending.

I think this level of specialization works for him for three reasons. One: Matt is a boy who loves basketball. He has a natural interest in the game. Two: Matt is under no pressure from his parents to be a great basketball player. They aren't looking for a payoff later in the form of an athletic scholarship or a coveted spot on his high school team. Matt wants to improve his skills and receive extra coaching for his own satisfaction and love of the game. Three: Matt gets a long break from organized, structured play. He also plays baseball and football with his friends. He enjoys swimming at the community pool. This is a well-rounded, healthy boy.

There are kids like Matt who do thrive and excel at their sport with more practice, more play, and more game time. But these kids are the minority. In my experience, many kids who specialize in sports before the age of thirteen burn out by the time they reach puberty. If Matt played in a spring league at a local sports arena or went to a longer four-week summer camp, he might, in fact, start to burn out on basketball. Kids burn out because more, more, and more over the years can simply become too much.

The point for every sports parent to know and believe: She doesn't have to play all the time in order to get good at a sport. If she does play all the time, she might get burned out or injured and leave the sport for good.

40. Weigh the pros and cons of the all-star or travel team

There are pros and cons to the elite travel and all-star teams. Elite teams can be positive *when they're in-season* for kids who are talented, love playing, and thrive on competition. I think it can be healthy and fun for kids who are good to have the opportunity to play against other kids who are also really good. Setting a goal, like making the elite team, can be a positive motivator for kids, as long as Mom and Dad have a healthy and balanced attitude about it. You don't want your child's world to be crushed if she doesn't make the elite team. It's much less likely to be devastating if you're grounding her every step of the way with statements like, "It will be great if you make the team, but there's always next year if you don't. Just give it your best, that's what counts the most."

It's when these elite teams play out of the traditional season and your child begins to play more than one season of the same sport that he becomes vulnerable to the common pitfalls of specialization, like overuse injuries and burnout. However, many elite teams do play in the traditional season so your child can still take a good break during the rest of the year.

You should also consider the time, money, and energy that being on the travel team will cost your entire family. One mom told me when her son was invited to join the all-star team in his town, she hung up the phone and thought, "Great! He made it." But then she realized that with three school-age children all playing sports, the all-star team simply was too much time and money to invest in one child's sport.

Critics feel that these teams cater to the elite and ignore the other kids playing the sport. Their fear is that the kids who don't make the all-star team will feel ostracized and develop self-esteem problems. I don't think it's appropriate to deny kids the opportunity to play at a more competitive level simply because other children will be left out. There are kids who make the high school team and kids who don't. That's the way it's always been in youth sports.

Sports parents have a lot to do with helping kids who don't make the team feel okay about it. When the parent makes a big deal out of the elite team or wants the child to have a place on the team for status, it creates problems for the child. Again, when Mom and Dad are balanced and have a positive attitude about making the team, chances are the child will too.

One dad who came to me was angry because the elite team in his community was highly politicized. It had become "It's not how well you play, but who you know" that would get you on the team. I hear this complaint a lot from moms and dads all over the country. To make it an even sorer point, these elite teams are often the ones who get the sponsors and the lion's share of the money over the recreational leagues.

This politicization is unfortunate. Your child deserves a place on the team, but life isn't always fair. Helping your child understand and move on in a positive way will do him a lot more good than constantly reinforcing the message, "You've been cheated."

I told this dad, "You feel angry and cheated now. But will it really matter in five years? Is it really affecting your son's future as much as you're allowing yourself to believe it is?"

He didn't answer me, but I hope I helped him see this situation in new way.

41. Reevaluate your child's involvement periodically

Specialization creates its own momentum. Early on, the child plays one or two seasons of the sport; then, each year, his involvement escalates. By the time he's eleven, his parents have invested several hundred hours and quite a bit of money to nurture him along. But now, the other boys are starting to catch up physically and he has to work even harder to keep pace with them. So, instead of stepping back and reevaluating his involvement, his parents, unable to accept the loss of all the time and money already invested, get him a private trainer and another three weeks of summer camp.

On it goes . . . until one day the boy breaks down before a practice and says, "I can't take it anymore!" And there are the parents holding an empty bag of high hopes. This happens all the time.

If moms and dads aren't careful, the momentum of specialization can become a whirlwind that traps them and their children. The best way to prevent this from happening to your family is to stop the momentum of specialization before it starts going too fast. Stop and ask yourself, "Is this working for our family? Is this still a good thing for Jake? Is he at risk for an overuse injury?" Sit down and write down the pros versus the cons on a sheet of paper to help you make your decision.

You should ask Jake, "Are you still enjoying this? Do you want to keep playing? How are you feeling physically after you play?" Be open to hearing him, even if it's not what you want to hear.

If your child plays one sport all year-round, I would reevaluate his involvement at least twice a year. If your child is playing two or three seasons a year, reevaluate at least once a year—these are minimums. It can't hurt to reevaluate after each season.

If your child's participation is not yielding the same benefits, such as increased skill or playing time, don't escalate his participation. Here's what Cindy, a concerned soccer mom, experienced:

Tommy started playing soccer when he turned nine. He was really good, a natural. The coach told us if he continued to play and practice a lot, he might have a shot at the traveling team when he turned twelve. Tommy was thrilled at the possibility and so were we. By the time he was eleven, he was playing the whole school year with summers off. Suddenly, he started losing his game. He just wasn't playing as well as he used to. He was grumpy and fighting with his sister a lot more. Some of the parents on his rec team told us we should consider sending him to soccer camp over the summer. Then I met Dr. Fish at a PTA meeting. He recommended scaling back and giving Tommy a season off. He also said to reduce the amount of conditioning Tommy was doing on his own with weights. Dr. Fish told me that many parents find that with less practice and with only one or two seasons of play kids play better and get a renewed sense of energy and fun. It seemed counterintuitive that he would get better by playing less but we took Dr. Fish's advice because we were out of options. Tommy is now on the traveling team and doing great. He's one of the high scorers and his mood is light and fun again. During his team's break he will not play sports. He will just relax and play with his friends.

If after scaling back, your child is still not performing well or enjoying himself, remind yourself of the many benefits your child has reaped. Tell yourself, "It's time to let Jake move on and try something new."

This will be much easier for you to do if you begin nurturing your child's sporting career with limited expectations that he will one day emerge a superior athlete. You may be disappointed to see him stop playing. A lot of parents are. But the sports parents who have the healthiest relationships with their children get over their disappointment. They recognize that sometimes things don't always work out the way they want them too. They are able to realize that good things can still come out of a situation, even if it doesn't yield the expected results.

Try to get your child to see the positives as well. Be honest. One dad had the wisdom to tell his son, "We made a mistake in pushing you to continue through this last season. We thought we were doing the best by you, but clearly, you're not happy playing soccer anymore. It's only natural that you don't want to play anymore. I wouldn't want to play if it felt like a job. We don't blame you and we hope you don't blame us. We all still got a lot out of it. We had good times and met nice families. You played on the travel team for two seasons and that was a unique experience. We're proud of you for doing so well."

42. Watch for burnout

When you were a kid, did you know even one child who got burned out on a sport? Probably not. Twenty years ago, there was no specialization in youth sports for the majority of kids. There was no year-round play. There were no indoor leagues or recreational teams. There were no elite or traveling teams. Thus, there was no burnout.

Specialization is a more recent development that we're only now beginning to understand. Because they never had to deal with it and didn't know any other kids who did, many parents are confused when confronted by their child's burnout. Many don't see it coming and others don't recognize it when it hits.

Burnout is the athlete's natural response to chronic, ongoing stress. It's that "I just can't take it anymore" feeling. Burnout causes young athletes to stop playing a sport because it's just not fun any longer. Young athletes who burn out tell me they feel like they had no say or control in their lives. One twelve-year-old boy told me, "I feel like an ice hockey machine."

Burnout among young athletes is clearly on the rise. Any child who specializes is at risk. Specialized sports play requires long periods of intense concentration and focus. How do you feel after long periods of intense concentration? You probably feel as if you need a break. The same is true for children. They need a break from the emotional stress and pressure created by so much practice, performance, competition, and dealing with coaches. And if they don't get the respite, they will eventually burn out.

It's tempting to think because sports is fun, kids experience a different kind of pressure, one that they're better able to tolerate.

It's not different. Stress is stress. Pressure is pressure. Burnout is burnout.

If your child is a specialized athlete, I urge you to assess the risk for burnout. Your child is at risk if he or she:

- **Isn't having fun anymore.** Kids describe the feeling to me as, "I'm not having any fun," "I'm sick of it," or "It feels like a job." Kids who aren't having fun will complain, avoid practicing, or fake illness rather than play.

- **Overtrains.** A child who practices, drills herself, or conditions by weight lifting or running every day or four to five days a week is overtraining. Eventually her body and mind will give out due to wear and tear. Kids who overtrain are highly susceptible to burnout.

- **Has trouble adjusting to different coaching styles.** It can be stressful to go from one coach to another as a child moves from one season to the next. One can make demands or have a style that varies sharply from another. Keeping up and dealing with the differences places kids under pressure.

- **Expects too much from himself.** Some kids don't understand that it really is okay to make a mistake or to have a bad game. The more perfectionist the child, the greater the pressure, and the greater the chances of burnout.

- **Is being pressured to perform well by Mom/Dad/Coach.** Again, the more pressure, the greater the chance that the child is stressed and not having fun.

- **Trains intensely in isolation.** One-on-one training is common for young athletes in sports like figure skating, gymnastics, diving, and tennis. But kids can feel socially isolated and lonely. There is limited contact with other young athletes to share the experience. This isolation can be enormously stressful.

Burnout is the kind of thing that parents don't see coming. They think: "That won't happen to Alex" or "We're not pressuring Sandy, so she'll be okay."

43. Have your child take a season off—whether or not he or she wants it

The best way to prevent burnout in a child who plays one sport is to mandate at least one nonplaying season a year. Give your child a break from this sport, whether or not she's asking for one. Encourage her to try another sport or to take up a noncompetitive sport like hiking or biking. You want her to stay active but you have to draw the line at year-round play in one sport.

Some kids will fight you on this decision. Many times, it's not Mom and Dad who want the child to play sports year-round, the child truly wants to play sports all the time. I hear this a lot from parents. The child seems obsessed and the parent isn't sure what would be better, letting her continue or making her drop out. Parents often ask me, "What do we do if we think she's fine now but may be heading for burnout down the road?"

Trina, a twelve-year-old gymnast told me, "I love gymnastics. I'm nuts about it. It's the only sport I ever liked." However, Trina's parents worried that her early morning practices with a private coach two mornings a week, afternoon workouts four days a week with the club team, and then her gymnastics camp in the summer were simply putting her under too much pressure, both physically and mentally, and taking up all of her time.

I told them that deciding that Trina needed a break, even if they weren't convinced her gymnastic participation was causing her immediate stress, was an option for them. Giving a child a break can be a good preventative against burning out in the future.

"You're the parents," I reminded them. "You make the decisions about what's best for your child because children can't do this for themselves."

Once in a while, especially if you're unsure that your child's sports participation is too much, it can be a good idea to have your child take a season off. Unlike when we were kids, if your daughter skips the fall soccer league she can usually join an indoor team for the winter, so it will not be an entire year before she can play again.

How your child reacts to the break will give you some idea if it's a good idea to cut back in general or cut back even more the next year. Some kids don't even know they're stressed out or physically or emotionally tired until they stop playing and take a break. That's when they realize how caught up they've been in the sport or how tired they've become. They start to see their friends again. They play different kinds of sports and games or even pickup games in their sport. At the end of the break, they seem rested and relaxed. That's a good indication that a regular break is appropriate for your child. Some parents are more comfortable with every other season or two seasons on and one off. You'll have to find the best fit for your child, but the most important point is for sports parents to realize that taking a season or two off is always an option.

During a child's break season, she can still stay aerobically ready to play sports but don't forget, kids need adequate rest to stay physically and mentally prepared to play sports.

V
• • • • • • • • • • •

COACHING CONCERNS:

Cultivate a positive relationship

Your child's coach will spend a lot of time working with your boy or girl. A coach is an authority figure to a child because he or she is in a position of power over your child. A coach will control how and when your child plays his or her sport. Regardless of your son's or daughter's age, the coach is in control of the game and is the one who calls the shots. Therefore your child's coach will have a good deal of influence over your son or daughter. Your goal as a concerned parent is to find the best match in a coach for your child. In some instances, such as recreational leagues and hiring private coaches for sports like tennis and gymnastics, you'll be able to be part of the coaching selection. But in many cases, such as high school sports, you won't have a say about who coaches your child. Either way, your goal is to have a positive relationship with the coach. Here are nine ways you can help your child successfully deal with this important person in his or her life.

44. Find the best coach for your child, not the best coach

When it comes to choosing a coach, many well-intentioned parents think, "I want to find someone with all the right coaching qualities." Moms and dads will often approach me with a list from a book they've read to ask me, "Are there any other qualities that I should be looking for besides experience, knowledge, a good feedback style . . . ?"

Rather than focus on the best qualities in a coach, which will vary from expert to expert anyway, focus on finding a coach who is the best match for your child's personality and athletic needs.

Marissa and Tom interviewed three coaches before choosing one to coach their ten-year-old son on a recreational soccer team. "We chose this coach even though he lacked experience because he was so nurturing and fair," said Marissa. "But by the end of the season, we saw that the kids weren't really listening to him anymore. He didn't command their respect. Tory didn't learn any new soccer skills."

After discussing this coach's lack of control with some of the other parents, to their surprise, Marissa and Tom learned that some of the parents were signing their kids up for another season with the same coach. These sports parents felt that their children had had a good experience on his team.

As Marissa and Tom learned, no two coaches are the same and no two sets of parents will have the same reaction to a coach. No two coaches will have all of the same qualities, philosophies, and experience. Sports parents are better off asking themselves, "What does Jeffrey need right now in a coach to have a good experience in hockey?" and work from there.

For children in elementary school, or under the age of eleven, it is particularly important to find a good match in a coach. These kids are in their formative years—they don't yet have the self-esteem and confidence they will need to navigate through difficult experiences on their own. That's why you want to ensure that the coach is someone your child will feel comfortable with and trust. If kids in their formative years have a positive experience with their coaches, they are likely to keep playing sports into their teen years and beyond. Once kids turn twelve and thirteen, they don't take things as personally if a coach has a bad day and yells at them or criticizes their performance. Up until the age of twelve, err on the side of caution. Do your best to find someone your child will feel safe and comfortable playing for. Focus on making a good match rather than on finding all the good qualities of a coach.

Joan and Paul, for example, have a shy nine-year-old boy, Brian, who takes criticism very hard. For them, it was more important to find a coach with a positive style of giving feedback rather than one who knew all of the finer points of the game.

As your child ages, what she needs in a coach may change. A child who thrived with an easygoing coach at the age of ten, does better with a coach who emphasizes discipline when she's thirteen. Some kids thrive with coaches who are authoritarian and sterner as opposed to the sensitive kind. Both types of coaches can be effective as long as your child trusts and respects the person. Again, it will depend upon what your child needs and what works for her.

45. Evaluate each perspective coach

When deciding on a coach, you should do the following:

- **Watch the coach in action.** You know the saying, "Actions speak louder than words . . ." Notice how she treats her own players and the other team. Does she give encouragement? Does she get angry if someone makes a mistake? What actions does she take if there's a problem?

- **Talk to other moms and dads.** Speak with other parents who have kids who've played for the coach. Find out what their experiences have been. Ask if they've had problems or issues with the coach, and if so, how was the situation resolved?

- **Interview the coach.** Speak one on one with the coach and find out his or her philosophies on issues like playing time, giving feedback, and discipline. There is no right or wrong answer. There is no right or wrong personality type. You will have to consider what you think is most important and valuable for your child. For example, one set of parents didn't choose a baseball coach because he believed that every child should play every position. These parents felt that their child was a talented infielder who would do best by playing second base exclusively. Another set of parents thought this coach was a good match for their son because the boy didn't yet know what position he liked best. They thought that playing on this team would help him explore the possibilities.

- **Get a sense of how open the coach is to hearing about your daughter's personality and experience with the sport.** Does he seem interested in learning about your child from you? This is important. You know your child the best and a coach who understands and respects your perspective is one who will be willing to work with you. For example, you can tell the coach, "Sally doesn't like to be corrected in front of the other girls. It makes her feel self-conscious. Do you have a problem with giving feedback in private?"

- **Go with your gut.** Choosing the right coach for your child is part doing your homework and part taking a leap of faith. The most important question you can ask yourself is: "Do I feel this person is someone I can talk to if a problem or issue arises?" It often will come down to your personal comfort level with the person. And that's fine. Personality has a lot to do with it. Too often, parents tell me, "I just had a feeling we were going to have problems . . . I should have listened to what that little voice was telling me."

- **Reevaluate periodically.** Often you won't know if it's a good match until the match is actually made. Talk to your child about his experience on the team. Ask him questions like, "What do you think of Coach?" "Is he helping you?" and "Are you having fun?" The answers will give you the best idea if your child is having a good experience with the coach.

46. Treat your child's coach the same way you would treat his teacher

I sat near a dad at my daughter's soccer game who got up twice and interrupted the coach while the game was in play. I don't know what his issue was, but unless he was worried that his daughter's health was in danger (which clearly wasn't the case), he should not have interrupted the coach. You would never barge into your child's classroom to give his teacher advice or to argue about the fairness of a grade, would you? Of course not. You would either telephone her or make an appointment to speak with her. You recognize that not only is this approach common courtesy to the teacher, you would never want to embarrass your child in front of his classmates.

Yet, every day parents go walking, running, or charging onto the field or court to give the coach advice or to argue with him or her. Every day, parents show disrespect to the coach and embarrass their kids—two things you would never do in your child's classroom. Even if you're calm and polite, it's still inappropriate to approach the coach during a game unless it's an extreme situation, such as if an official or another player is verbally abusing your child. Otherwise, stay off the field!

Once kids are in their teenage years, they would rather evaporate into the air than watch their parents get into a discussion or argument with their coach during a game. One thirteen-year-old girl put it this way: "I feel like I'm going to throw up when I see my mom bugging the coach."

If you have a problem or an issue with the coach, the time to discuss it is not during or immediately after the game. Emotions are running high for you both. Wait until you're home and have calmed down. Then call the coach and let her know that you'd like to speak with her about an issue. Ask, "What would be a good time for you to talk?"

Be respectful of the fact that many coaches are not paid. They are taking time out of their busy lives to work with your child. They don't have the time to sit around and talk endlessly about every child on the team.

When a sports parent treats his child's coach with the same respect that he treats his teachers, there is a good chance that the relationship will be a positive and healthy one.

47. Advocate for your child—but set limits

A dad of one of my son's teammates was always speaking with the coach and giving him advice before and after games. I once saw him practically chasing the coach off the field. Another time, I saw the coach purposefully avoid this dad by ducking behind some bleachers.

Frankly, many parents are too quick to speak with their coach about a problem or an issue. Parents today are so eager to ensure that their children are being treated fairly that they often overadvocate. Parents often do this because they feel that their own parents perhaps didn't advocate for them enough. They think, "Well, Sean isn't going to have to put up with what I did!" Some parents try to intervene with the coach because they've bought into the "more in sports is better" myth that I discuss in the previous chapter. They think that unless their child plays every game that he will be at a disadvantage. For this reason, the issue of playing time is one of the biggest areas of contention between coaches and parents.

Though their concern comes from the heart, parents who are too quick to run to the coach with a complaint in the end often don't serve their children's best interests. First of all, you don't want your child to learn to frequently take an adversarial position or to feel that she has to be on the alert for getting cheated or mistreated in youth sports. This kind of attitude can take the fun out of sports for kids. It is helpful for kids to understand that they are not always going to like their coaches or what their coaches do, but that they can still have a good overall experience on the team.

Second, if you frequently approach the coach, the coach is

probably going to end up resenting you. Do you like it when people tell you how to do your job or raise your child? Probably not. Some coaches even take their resentment out on your child. For example, it's time to put a new wide receiver in the game. There are two equal players but because Paul's dad has been bugging the coach about giving the boy more field time, the coach sends in David, whose dad never engages him in discussion.

Your goal should be to find the middle ground in advocating for your child with the coach. Here are four ways to help you find this middle ground:

- **Believe the coach is a good person.** Most coaches truly enjoy working with and helping young people—that's why they sacrifice their time for little or no compensation. Most coaches try to be fair. Begin your relationship with this assumption that "Coach Brady is going to try to do a good job," and not a more adversarial one like, "I'm going to make sure this coach does right by Jeannie."

- **Don't speak up until you see a pattern.** I know it can be hard to bite your lip. I had to bite mine the other day at my son's baseball game. I know Ari likes playing infield and for the second game in a row the coach had him in the outfield. But I also know this coach has always been fair in rotating the players. I realize that he can't be exactly fair each game. It's the big picture that matters. If Ari was in the outfield for the next four games or the better part of the season, then there would be a pattern and I would probably mention it to the coach. Likewise, if a coach snaps her feedback at your child once or twice, I wouldn't make a big issue out of it. Your child is not going to be irreparably damaged by infrequent behavior of that kind. However, if it happens three or four times, you should speak up and say, "Coach, the last four times Jeannie made a mistake, you spoke harshly to her. She's much more able to take criticism when you speak to her calmly. Can you do that?"

- **Give the coach time to get to know your child.** In the beginning of the season, the coach is learning about your child and your child is learning about the coach. You may be concerned by disorganization, inequity of playing time, or the coach's feedback style, but give it at least a few weeks or games. Usually, these kinds of issues work out by mid-season. If they don't, you would be perfectly within your rights to talk to the coach.

- **Check in with an assistant coach or some of the other parents.** If you're not sure whether or not there's a problem, ask one of the assistant coaches or some other sports parents for their opinion. I've done this myself. I've approached the assistant coach and have asked a question like, "Is the coach changing his policy on rotating the players?" Or I might ask another parent, "Does it seem like Coach isn't rotating the kids as much as he used to?" Talking to other parents and/or assistant coaches can help you ascertain whether or not there's really an issue you need to discuss with the coach.

48. Learn how to successfully deal with authoritarian-style coaches

Though coaches come in all kinds of personality types you will find many authoritarian-style coaches in youth sports. These coaches are more common once your child reaches high school. At this level, coaches are usually paid professionals with experience and definite opinions about how the game should be played and how to get the best out of kids. An authoritarian-style coach is one who believes, "It's my way or the highway." These coaches believe in applying lots of structure and discipline. They're not as soft-spoken and as easygoing as the volunteer coaches you encountered when your child was under the age of ten. They're also not as open to feedback as many parents would like.

These are the coaches who like to be the boss, and the ones who call the shots. This is not the same thing as a control freak or a tyrant. Authoritarian-style coaches, as long as they truly care about the well-being of your child, are not bad for your child. For example, I saw a tough coach bark orders at his team, but when one of the players on the opposing team acted inappropriately by intentionally elbowing an opposing player, the coach quickly intervened by speaking to the official. Though he was stern, he cared about his players. Often, young athletes blossom under the direction of a coach who makes them work hard, holds them accountable, and lets them know where they need to improve.

It is the parents who often have difficulty in dealing with authoritarian-style coaches. Parents worry that the coach is too tough or not nurturing enough. Speaking about her thirteen-year-old son's football coach, one mom told me, "He acts like a drill sergeant. He's always barking orders and making the boys do push-ups. I don't know if that's good for William."

"Does William mind?" I asked. "Does he seem to enjoy being on the team?"

"Oh yes," she said. "He really likes his coach. But I just worry that he's too hard on the boys."

This is very common—moms and dads worry about a coach's being too tough but the child is having a good experience. I've even been through this myself. One of my son's coaches is quite the authoritarian. He's very strict and can be pretty tough when he gives feedback. At first I didn't think Eli would do very well with him. I worried that he would find the coach too tough. But I was wrong. Eli is very happy on his team. He respects and trusts his coach even though he doesn't always like everything the coach says and does. That's because this coach has proven that he's fair by giving all the players a shot at playing during games, has erred on the side of caution if there's an injury, and has gotten to know the boys as individuals. That's why Eli can take the good and leave the rest.

As parents, we want the other adults in our children's lives to be nurturing and positive, especially when delivering criticism to our kids. But all of the adults in your young athlete's life aren't going to be as nurturing as you are. They're not always going to balance a criticism with a supportive statement. As long as your child respects the coach and feels like her coach ultimately has her best interest at heart, most kids will do well with an authoritarian-style coach. Many thrive. Some parents are surprised to discover that their kids respond very well to a tougher style coach. One dad told me, "Jordan really needed a kick in the butt and now he's doing better on the team and even in school."

So before you judge your child's coach too strict or too harsh, as long as your child seems to be doing well, give it some time. It could be that your buttons are getting pushed by hearing a coach bark orders and not your child's.

49. Teach your child to deal with the coach directly

When your child reaches high school age, he or she needs to learn how to self-advocate with the coach. Of course, if the coach is a particularly difficult person, or if there's an extreme situation, such as verbal abuse, your child will need your help in advocating. You don't want to announce, "That's it, you're on your own with Coach," but rather begin to teach your child to speak up. One of the benefits of youth sports is that it helps kids learn how to deal successfully with authority figures. The way they learn how to do this is by raising issues with the coach directly.

In beginning to get kids comfortable with speaking to their coaches, you can do the following:

- **Set a good example.** The way kids learn how to talk to adults and authority figures is by watching and hearing you. If you've spoken to the coach privately before, from this point on, you should include your child in the discussion or conversation. When it's over, talk to your child about what happened. Point out specifics like, "Did you notice that even though Coach seemed a little angry, I didn't get angry in return. Angry words don't help work out a solution." Or "I hope you saw that Coach and I were able to make a compromise about your playing time. Sometimes, we don't always get exactly what we ask for, but now at least if you keep up your end of the bargain and work harder, you'll be on the field more."

- **Let your child know he or she has a right to speak up.** You think your child knows this, but in fact, he often *doesn't* know it's okay to speak up to an adult. For most of your child's life, he's been taught to listen to adults and perhaps has even been discouraged from questioning them. Kids need permission to confront authority figures.

- **Acknowledge that it's not always easy to speak up.** Think about how you feel when asking your boss for a raise. You feel nervous. Kids feel nervous too. Let them know, "It's okay to feel nervous before talking to Coach, but you'll get more comfortable the more times you do it" or "You may feel some butterflies in your stomach when you talk to Coach Jones and that's okay. The important thing is to speak up, even when you feel nervous."

- **Talk about the timing.** Tell Becky that the best time to talk to her coach is not right after they've lost the game or when there are a lot of people around. Let her know that she shouldn't confront her coach when either one of them is angry or upset. Tell her to wait until she calms down and then privately she can ask: "Coach, I'd like to talk to you. Do you have a few minutes now or is later better?"

- **Teach your child to stick to specifics.** Your child perceives that, "Coach never compliments me," or "She's always picking on me," but you need to remind her not to approach a conversation this way. "Always" and "never" will only put the coach on the defensive because they are accusing words. Instead, encourage your child to be specific about what her issue is:

ACCUSING: *You always yell at me.*
SPECIFIC: *When you yelled at me after the last two mistakes I made, it made me feel worse.*

ACCUSING: *You never let me play.*
SPECIFIC: *I've only played for five minutes in the last three games.*

- **Role-play with your child.** One of the biggest reasons that even parents get uncomfortable talking with coaches is because they don't know what to say. Adults gets tongue-tied and so do kids. The next time your ten- or eleven-year-old complains, "I like playing the infield, but Coach has had me in the outfield for the last three games," give him some possible ways to bring it up to the coach. First tell him, "Bobby, I'm sure that Coach doesn't realize you're unhappy in the outfield. Why don't you discuss it with him?" Then rehearse some ways he can approach the coach on his own and respond to him using the following scenarios for inspiration:

BOBBY: *Coach, I really like playing the infield. Do you think the next game I can play second base?*

or

BOBBY: *Coach, is there something I can be doing or practicing to get more time at second base?*

Then discuss what the coach might say and how Bobby might respond.

COACH: *You know I like everyone to rotate positions each game.*
BOBBY: *Well, I'm sure you didn't realize it, but I've played the outfield for the last three games.*

or

COACH: *The last time you played second base you made three errors. You're more valuable to me in the outfield.*
BOBBY: *I would really like the chance to play second base again. If I spend the next few weeks practicing extra hard, will you give me another chance?*

- **Discuss the outcome with your child.** Your child needs to understand that just because she was brave and spoke up, she still might not get her way. This happens sometimes. But discuss what she did get out of it—the knowledge that she stood up for herself in a positive way. Let her know that sometimes she and Coach will have to agree to disagree. Remind her that she still took an important step in advocating for herself and that counts.

50. Work with your child's coach to ensure a positive recruitment process

When a talented athlete is in the tenth or eleventh grade, he or she often begins to attract interest from coaches from colleges and universities. As I discuss in chapter 4, Specialization, the competition to win athletic scholarships is intense.

If your son or daughter gets calls and letters, indicating the interest of recruiting coaches, the recruitment process can be exciting, even glamorous, at first. Some athletes are invited to special sports camps for the purpose of being scouted by college coaches. It's very prestigious. It's exciting to get letters and phone calls of interest from coaches all over the country. However, the recruitment process can quickly become a black hole of time, energy, and emotions for hopeful athletes and their families. With the cost of college becoming more prohibitive each year, more athletes are vying even just for the attention of the university and college coaches, let alone a tryout, let alone a scholarship. In boys' high school basketball alone, out of over 540,000 players, there are only an estimated 4,500 freshman positions available (source: National Collegiate Athletic Association).

Unfortunately, some parents get caught up in the status element of recruitment. They go to games and tell the other parents, "We got a letter from such and such university yesterday." If you find that your own ego is on the line when it comes to your boy or girl getting recruited, I urge you to review numbers 8 and 22 for advice. Parents need to handle the recruiting process calmly so that they don't pressure their kids or allow recruiting coaches to do so either. You can't be your child's advocate if your own wants and needs are getting mixed up with what's best for your son or daughter.

The first step in ensuring a positive recruitment process is to formulate a game plan with your child's coach. The key to successfully implementing this game plan is understanding what your job and role are, what the coach's job and role are, and work from there. Your job is to be a parent and advocate. You need to make sure no prospective coach tries to unfairly influence or pressure your child. Your job is also to help your child see the big picture (i.e., "It's not the end of the world if you're not recruited") and to stay calm and focused in nerve-racking, high-pressure tryout games. (See points 15 to 18 on managing competitive stress and point 31 on visualization techniques.)

The coach's job is to help initiate and field contact with college coaches, offer advice about the best match for your child, and to coach your child in the game. This may sound like a no-brainer, but one of the biggest obstacles in a positive recruitment process is often an eager, well-meaning parent giving his child conflicting advice on strategy and performance. It's the coach's job to dictate what your son or daughter does during a game, not yours.

Manuel was a point guard with a good chance of getting an athletic scholarship. His job is to dribble up and distribute the ball. Right before a tryout game, his coach told him, "Think, 'pass first, shoot second.' " But his dad, wanting his son to get noticed, told his son, "Think, 'shoot first, pass second.' " Manuel was caught in the middle. It was a tough situation for the boy. After the first quarter, Manuel's dad and his coach had a heated discussion. The coach pointed out, "He's going to be recruited as a point guard, so let's showcase him as a point guard, not as a shooting guard." Manuel's father was able to understand the coach's reasoning and he backed off of his advice. (In the end, Manuel did get a scholarship.)

Hopefully, you've formed a positive relationship with your child's high school or club coach from the beginning. Of course, there are exceptions. You may feel your child's coach isn't promoting your child enough or to her best advantage. One mother threatened to pull her daughter out of the school for her senior year because she felt the coach would jeopardize her daughter's chances of getting a scholarship. This had been an acrimonious relationship for two years. Fortunately, the mother was able to temporarily reconcile her differences with the coach in order to get through the recruitment process. Though that's an extreme example, you do need to work with your child's coach, no matter what your personal opinion about him or her may be. You may have to put your personal feelings aside in order to act in the best interest of your child.

Here are three more key points to keep in mind:

- The coach's advice and strategy have helped your child get to this point. She wants your child to win the scholarship too. When their players go off and play at the college level with an athletic scholarship it's good for the coach's reputation and track record. Most coaches are not going to "blow it" when a recruiting coach is in attendance by keeping your child on the bench or by giving him bad direction.

- You need to become educated about the process and learn the rules of conduct for recruiting coaches. You can contact the National Collegiate Athletic Association (NCAA) to request a free brochure on recruiting rules and other information (800-638-3731 or www.ncaa.org). You should also speak to other parents who have gone through the process. They can offer you inside advice and guidance.

- For parents who don't necessarily have the stars, but do have above-average athletes (the more common situation), you can work on your child's behalf to get the attention of college coaches. The reality is that it's tough to get the attention of college coaches with so many kids playing high school sports. You and your child may be disappointed by a lack of interest. You may think your daughter has a chance if only you could get her in front of some college coaches. My advice is to play it out. When parents act thoughtfully and within reason, it can be good to see if you can generate some interest on your own. I define "within reason" as sending out ten videotapes and letters to perspective coaches and not a hundred. Go forward with the attitude, "Let's see what happens. At least we'll know we tried." (See number 38 for additional advice on keeping your expectations realistic.) You should approach the coach and ask for assistance in putting together a highlight tape and a list of contacts. Most coaches will help parents and athletes if they are asked.

51. Form a parents' group

Though I truly believe that the majority of coaches are good and generous people, I have heard of some extreme cases in which a coach was inept, unfair, or even verbally and emotionally abusive to the players. I saw a coach at a Little League game who had to be removed from the field by the umpire because he was cursing and screaming at the other team's coach. He didn't yell at his players, but such behavior is unacceptable. The coach is a role model for your child.

If your child's coach proves to be one of the extreme cases, you should make every effort to speak with the coach to let him or her know that, "It's not okay to keep Jenny on the bench every game" or "I won't allow you to yell at Scott for making mistakes."

If talking with the coach in private fails to produce a change in behavior consider going to a higher authority. A public or private school will have an athletic director, while a community team or recreational league always has a director.

When approaching a higher athletic authority, you will have more clout if you go, not as a single concerned parent, but as a group of concerned parents. Let's face it, unless there are already numerous complaints against the coach, you could look like an overzealous sports parent. Chances are, if the coach is bad enough for you to consider going over his or her head, other parents will have similar concerns. Take the initiative and organize the other moms and dads. Appoint one person to be the spokesperson for the parents. That way when you have a meeting there won't be a dozen people talking at once. Draft a letter of complaint documenting the specific issues or situations and have all of the parents sign it. It will be much harder for a school principal or a league director to ignore eight sets of parents than it would be to ignore one set. The other advantage of a forming a parent group is that it will keep the coach from singling out one child and minimizing her playing time or otherwise retaliating against her. When parents are persistent and use their power as a group, positive results are more likely to result.

52. As a last resort, take your child off the team

You did all the right things—you found the middle ground in advocating for your child, you were respectful of the coach, you spoke with her at her convenience—but still you feel the coach is not being fair about playing time or she continues to speak harshly to your child. What do you do?

You may have to pull your child off the team. Before you do that, however, I would make every effort to help your child stay on the team, especially if it's mid-season or beyond. As long as your child is not being verbally or emotionally abused, it can be worth sticking it out, especially if your child is having a good experience in other ways. You can use the situation as an opportunity to help your child learn how to successfully deal with a difficult authority figure. Here's how Maryanne encouraged her daughter to stay on her team:

> We tried to get Coach to give you more playing time but she clearly has her own way of running the team. Even though we don't think it's fair, we still think that you're getting a lot out of being on the team. You've made lots of friends and you have so much fun at practice. Let's try not to focus on the bad and focus on the good.

If, however, your child is anxious, depressed, or otherwise in distress about continuing on the team because of the coach's behavior, or if the coach's behavior is abusive, I would pull your child from the team. A coach does have some degree of power over your child, no matter what her age. By keeping her on the team you risk sending the wrong message: "It's okay for authority figures to behave any way they want" or "Authority figures are allowed to treat you badly."

That's certainly not the message you want to give your child. You should discuss this experience with your child to let him know that things don't always work out. For example:

> DAD: *We know how much you love basketball and hate to leave the team. But we can't allow you to play for your coach. He's verbally abusive. It isn't acceptable for anyone to speak to you using curse words. Sometimes, there isn't anything we can do to change another person's behavior and we have to walk away. Let's see if we can find a recreational team for you to play with next season.*

Though parents worry that pulling their child off a team will somehow cause the young athlete to fall behind, I think it's more detrimental to leave a child in distress on a team. With year-round play available for so many sports, your child won't have to wait another year to play his or her sport again. Your child has options through community and recreational programs outside of school to work with more positive coaches.

53. Be aware of the special issues of coaching your own child

I used to love soccer and then my dad had to go and be the coach. Now, all he talks to me about is soccer. We used to talk about all sorts of stuff.

—Jeremy, age nine

Coaching your own child can be a great experience. You can spend more time with your child, develop a common bond, get to know his friends better, and provide a valuable volunteer service in your community. All great things.

However, coaching your own child can also be an opportunity to go overboard. Parents who coach sometimes give their kids too much feedback or focus too much on the sport. Your relationship with your child could become strained.

Follow these five guidelines to make your coaching of her team a positive experience:

- **Treat her teammates with respect.** Your daughter will see your behavior with her teammates as a direct reflection on her. And she's right. If you yell at her friends for making mistakes, they will probably take it out on her in one form or another. Your child could withdraw out of embarrassment. Treat all the kids on the team with kindness and respect.

- **When pointing out your son's errors in front of others, be respectful.** I've seen parent coaches yell at or criticize their own kids simply because they can. I don't think they mean to harm their kids, but the outcome can be damaging. Kids don't like to be singled out in front of others. Kids don't want to be embarrassed in front of others. Treat your child the same way you treat the other kids on the team—with respect.

- **Leave the game on the field.** When you're in the car on the way home from the game or at the dinner table don't talk about mistakes your daughter made or how disappointed you are that the team didn't win. Be a mom or a dad, not a coach.

- **Keep coaching issues to yourself.** One dad I know used his son as a sounding board for his ideas and criticisms of other players. This became a burden for the boy. He was ten years old and didn't want to help his dad make decisions about who should play what position.

- **Make sure your entire relationship is not based upon sports.** Make a point to engage in nonsports activities with your child. This will show her that you care about her and are interested in her life outside the team.

VI

· · · · · · · · · · · ·

SIBLING RIVALRY:

Foster a healthy competitive environment

Rivalry can be a positive motivator in sports, as it was for basketball legends Magic Johnson and Larry Bird. They pushed each other to excel since they first met as opponents in college. Their rivalry, though fierce, was always underscored by respect and friendship.

When your child has another child to play against, he can test and compare his skills and challenge himself to improve. When those rivals are siblings, however, there is an added dimension of complexity. While sibling rivalry in sports is often a positive motivator for kids, it can turn negative. Siblings don't always compete simply to challenge themselves, improve, or even win; they often compete for their parents' attention or for dominance over the other.

When sibling rivalry turns negative, it can in its mildest form mean occasional teasing or taunting. At its worst, kids can appear to become mortal enemies when competing. I've had many moms and dads tell me stories about brothers or sisters who normally get along fairly well but who act like they hate each other when playing any kind of sports.

Don't panic. Kids go in and out of competitive phases with siblings. Plus, there are many proactive steps moms and dads can take to foster a healthy competitive relationship between their children.

54. Understand that siblings aren't just competing to win the game

Your kids aren't just competing to score a point or win a game. They're also competing for your attention, love, approval, and respect. Kids want the "bragging rights" that they've won the big game or scored the big point. They want to be the one to say, "I won" or "I'm faster than Harry" at the dinner table. Kids often believe that if they win and excel at sports they will get special attention from Mom and Dad. Oftentimes, to complicate matters, they do get the extra attention they're seeking.

It's important to be aware of the verbal and nonverbal messages you send to your children about their sports accomplishments. Your message might be a positive one, such as, "Winning is great, it's fun to win, but a game is only a game" or "Sports is important but so is music, art, and family game night." But your message might also be one that encourages negative competition between your children if you reward or emphasize winning. Two brothers told me that whichever one of them won in sports would get extra dessert after dinner. No wonder they were so competitive with one another. The message their parents sent was: The winner gets rewarded and the loser doesn't.

Parents foster sibling rivalry when they make comments such as, "Danny doesn't have to do the dishes tonight because he was the star at basketball today." Even just making Danny's sports feat the center of the family discussion at dinner can cause his brothers and sisters to feel left out, not as special, and not as loved by Mom and Dad. Or, if Mom or Dad is an especially enthusiastic sports fan who gets very excited by Danny's accomplishments there is the danger that the other children will feel that the only way to Mom's or Dad's heart is through sports. That's why it's important to be equally enthusiastic and give equal airtime to all your children's accomplishments, whether sports-related or not.

You can, and should, acknowledge one child's sports accomplishments. But if you give the sibling who wins or excels at sports too much extra attention and special treatment, you make it more likely that your children will engage in unhealthy competition, whether that gets played out in the driveway basketball court or who gets to ride in which seat in the car.

Rarely do parents set out to encourage negative competitive feelings between their children. But it's very easy to do so if you knowingly or unknowingly send the message that whoever wins will get more of Mom's and Dad's attention, approval, and love.

55. Foster a positive competitive environment

Many parents make the mistake of thinking that it's bad or unhealthy for siblings to have competitive feelings toward one another. Parents tell me things like, "The girls compete a lot" or "Every sport the boys play together becomes a competition" as if that competitiveness by its very nature is the problem. It isn't.

Bob and Elizabeth are parents of three girls who compete for everything—who gets to sit in the front seat, who is the best volleyball player, and who is Mom and Dad's favorite. Elizabeth asked me, "How do I stop getting them to compete?" and I answered, "You don't."

It's unrealistic for parents to think that they can eliminate competitive feelings between their children. Some degree of competition is perfectly healthy, normal, and unavoidable between siblings, especially siblings who play sports. What better place to start to figure out what your natural abilities and talents are than to stack yourself up against your brother or sister? And sports, because there is a score, because there is a winner and a loser, naturally encourage competition. There is almost always going to be some level of competition between sports-playing siblings. In fact, even if your kids get along extremely well or only occasionally argue, chances are if they're put into uniforms, sparks will fly.

What you, as the parent, need to do is judge whether or not your kids are engaged in negative competition. Negative competition is the underlying problem in most sports-related sibling-rivalry issues.

How will you know if your kids are competing negatively? Your first clue is the nature of the competitive environment between siblings. Negative competition has very high stakes. Every contest or competition is about dominance and superiority. Negative competition is often about proving something— that one sibling is a better person, is more powerful, or is the favored child. Negative competition becomes more than a game; it becomes a clash of wills, a fight for superiority and for the lion's share of Mom's and Dad's attention. No wonder the stakes can seem so high!

When siblings are competing in a negative manner it can take on a variety of forms.

If your kids are screaming and hitting each other before, during, or after a sports competition, that's a pretty solid indication that you've got negative competition going on. But negative competition can also cause kids to withdraw from normal activities and even cause changes in eating and sleeping habits.

Positive competition, on the other hand, is not about approval, dominance, or being better than one's sibling. Winning or being better than one's brother or sister is not the ultimate goal. Positive competition between siblings is about siblings helping one another reach their full potential and having a good time.

It's not the competitive feelings that you need to control— it's the way those feelings get expressed. If your kids are fighting and hitting each other after the hockey game then that is what you want to change. If your child suddenly starts having trouble sleeping after he or she has played sports or games with a sibling, then it's the negative competition causing him or her the stress that you need to deal with. It simply isn't possible or realistic to have children who are free from competitive feelings. It is possible, however, to have children who can learn how to compete in a positive competitive environment.

56. Know the eight warning signs of unhealthy sports-related sibling rivalry

Though some degree of competition between brothers and sisters is normal, you should know the eight warning signs of negative sibling competition. There may be a problem if you notice:

- **Abusive verbal behavior before, during, or after a competition or for a prolonged period of time following a sporting event or game.** One sibling tries to chip away at the other's self-confidence with name-calling, taunting, and teasing.

- **Hitting, punching, kicking, or other inappropriate physical behaviors.**

- **One sibling consistently performing worse against his or her sibling than he or she would perform in other competitive settings.** This pattern typically indicates that a significant level of pressure, worry, or stress is being set in motion by competing against one's sibling.

- **A marked personality change.** For example, the outgoing child becomes very reserved, or the reserved child starts to act out of control.

- **A change in eating habits, sleeping patterns, or interest level.** I often hear descriptions like, "Janie just isn't herself when she is playing or competing with her sister," when negative competition is fueling the rivalry. "Just isn't herself" typically means that there is something different or wrong with Janie that gets activated particularly when competing with her sibling.

- **Complaint of physical injury.** One frustrated mom said, "I wish I had a dollar for every time I've heard Joseph say, 'Jimmy hurt me,' and then Jimmy says, 'I never touched him.' " Incidents like this reflect the child's desire to opt out of competition with Jimmy. As I discuss in the next section, injury remains a socially acceptable way to opt out of competition.

- **Continual blowups between siblings that are out of proportion to the actual event that occurred.** Some parents describe it to me as, "Any competition can feel like life or death."

- **Avoidance of a sport or game with another sibling, even one he or she used to enjoy playing.**

If you notice any of the above warning signs occurring on a regular basis, you should intervene. It's not enough to simply break up the skirmishes, you need to teach your children how to compete in a more positive and healthy manner.

57. Look for "flash points" between competing siblings

Carol and Barry were worried about their two sons, Keith, age twelve, and Jeremy, age fourteen.

"The boys are always trying to beat each other at baseball, basketball, table tennis, diving, even horseshoes," said Carol. "They torment each other. They fight all the time. It's terrible."

I explained to Carol and Barry, as I do to most of the parents who come to me for help with sibling-rivalry problems, that Keith's and Jeremy's competitive issues might not be quite as serious as they had come to believe.

I did not mean to belittle Carol and Barry's problem or concerns. But as soon as I hear parents say "always," "all the time," and "at each other's throats constantly," to describe their sibling-rivalry situation, I know from years of experience that we might have to do some searching for the gray area—the area in which the brothers were really having a competition problem and the area in which they were competing well and getting along fine.

When siblings are having rivalry problems around sports, the problem can appear far worse to parents than it actually is. Even a few fights a week can be draining to a parent's energy. Parents often worry that if their children are in a phase where they argue all the time, "It will go on this way forever."

While this is often the way parents perceive the situation, please be reassured, it's rarely the case.

Before you can begin to help your kids get along better, you have to understand where they're having trouble competing positively. You've got to boil down the "boys fight all the time," to the specific situations that the boys don't compete well in, such as "the boys fight when they play basketball and when other children are playing sports with them." You've got to find what I call the "flash points." The flash points are those athletic, competitive situations that turn explosive. I'm not talking about when kids argue about whose turn it is to unload the dishwasher. The flash points are when you see the red flags in one or more of a child's behavior, such as verbal abuse or physical violence. Look for the true negative competitive situations and the details that contribute to or lead up to them.

Here are three things to keep in mind about flash points:

- **Flash points can be particular types of games.** Your kids fight during baseball, but not Ping-Pong. Running is a high-stakes event but not backyard volleyball.

- **Flash points can be particular to an individual child.** Does one get more frustrated when tired? Hungry? If competing right after a long day at school? After a bad day? On weekends versus weekdays? When a parent is watching? When certain friends are involved?

- **Negative competitive situations don't just come to life in one instant.** There's usually a buildup to an explosion, which often manifests itself physically in children. If you can help your child build awareness that it's happening, you can help him or her nip the explosion in the bud. Ask them, "Before you started fighting with your brother, did your palms sweat? Did you want to cry? Was your stomach in knots?" Try to discover what thoughts they were having that led to the explosion of negative competition. Simply ask, "What were you thinking when Abigail started to beat you?" It's okay to put some words into their mouths, especially for younger children. You can prompt them by asking, "Were you thinking, 'She always wins'? or 'I hate when she beats me?' " Once you understand what patterns the flash points take, you can then implement a more manageable "game plan"—one that's targeted to increase positive competition and reduce the likelihood of negative competition. Parents can help their kids avoid the flash points by helping them understand what they are. For example, if you notice that one of your children gets grumpy and irritable after school when the child is hungry, you can make sure he has a high-protein energy snack before engaging in after-school play. Let him know, "Before you play after school, you need to eat because when you're hungry you get irritable and you can't play well with your brother. So you need to tell me when you're getting hungry, okay?"

Another advantage to finding the flash points is that you'll discover the areas of positive competition as well as the negative ones. If your kids are simply going through a phase in which they're having trouble competing at anything, steer them toward physical activities in which there isn't necessarily going to be a score or a winner or loser, such as hiking, canoeing, weight lifting, or biking. Reinforce the idea that recreation and physical activity don't necessarily have a winner, a loser, or a score but can be about exercise and fun. I've encouraged parents to give siblings who were fierce sports rivals household chores they can complete together. One dad gave his bickering sons this common goal: Clean the garage out in two hours or less and I'll take you both out for ice cream sundaes. It worked. The boys teamed up, cleaned the garage, and got to share in their victory over banana splits.

If you don't think your kids are ready to play certain games, start them off in activities and games in which they have a history of cooperation—maybe sports-related, maybe not. If they can play cards and not fight, get them playing cards. The key is to get them out of the potentially explosive flash-point situation and into a situation where they can compete positively.

58. Confront the green-eyed monster head-on

Rival siblings feel many emotions toward each other—disappointment, frustration, anger, sadness—but often the core emotion at the center of the situation is jealousy.

Jealousy is a perfectly normal emotion, especially when one sibling is more talented in sports than the other. It's also quite common for younger siblings to be jealous of the talents and abilities of older siblings.

Though it's certainly natural, jealousy can be a very uncomfortable, shaming emotion for adults, let alone kids. It's so unpleasant we've actually nicknamed it "the green-eyed monster." Though many moms and dads prefer not to see this emotion in their children, it's best to confront it openly and honestly. Kids need help dealing with this powerful, often frightening, feeling.

Here are three things you can do to help a jealous child:

- **Don't show disapproval.** Adults are not proud of feeling jealous so they are often uncomfortable seeing it in their own children. Unfortunately, we translate this disapproval to our children. We tell kids: "It's not okay to feel jealous because your sister was picked for the soccer team and you weren't; you're supposed to be happy for her" or "It's not okay to feel jealous of the attention your track star brother gets." Kids get the message loud and clear and try to repress their unpleasant feelings because it's not okay with Mom or Dad. But it is okay to feel jealous; what isn't okay is when those jealous feelings are expressed in a competitive situation through taunting, teasing, and physical violence. This is the distinction that parents need to explain to kids.

- **Empathize with your child.** Your child shouldn't feel guilty for having a strong emotion like jealousy or anger toward a sibling. Instead, help her understand that feeling something doesn't make her a bad person; thinking something isn't the same as acting on it. You can say, "I understand that you feel disappointed when you lose to your sister" or "I know it's hard not to be able to run as fast as your sister." Don't lecture, just listen and then reflect back what your child is telling you: "What you're telling me is that you wish you could run as fast as Naomi." When children are ages ten and under, they need guidelines for understanding how people feel in certain situations. They need to be reassured that, "It's hard for John and Greta and even Daddy to feel like you can't do something as well as someone else. Everyone feels this way sometimes. The important thing is to do your best." Young children look up to their parents; they take their cues from them. By reassuring them that what they're feeling is normal, you take the mystery and scariness out of strong emotions like jealousy. Kids are able to calm down when they feel understood. At older ages, around sixteen and seventeen, you can remind your child that he's playing the game to have fun, not because he's trying to prove how well he can play. You can say, "Yes, Scott is a faster swimmer than you are but you are a terrific volleyball player. People are good at different things, it's just the way life is sometimes."

- **Remind your child that she has a range of emotions toward her sibling.** Just because one sibling is jealous of another, doesn't mean that negative feelings are the only feelings she has. Kids feel many positive feelings toward their siblings—like love, tenderness, and protectiveness. Many kids like the fact that they have a sibling to play with pretty much all the time. They just might not express these positive emotions as vocally and dramatically as they do the negative ones, especially in the heat of competition. When you remind a jealous child that she also cares about her sister, that she laughs with her and has many good times, it helps take the power away from an uncomfortable feeling. You can say, "Just this morning, you and Sheila were laughing together. Yesterday, you stuck up for her on the playground. You don't always feel jealous that she wins at tennis."

Parents who openly discuss feelings of jealousy with their children are helping them deal with a powerful and uncomfortable emotion. Kids who know how to handle jealousy can learn how to accept and channel their jealousy into something more positive. One dad challenged his ten-year-old not to try to be as good at pitching as his twelve-year-old brother, but to try to develop his hitting skills. The boy discovered that he was actually a very good hitter and no longer felt threatened by his brother's accomplishments as a pitcher.

59. Teach your children how to resolve their conflicts

You won't be there every minute or for every game. You can't always be present to head off trouble. This is why you need to teach your kids how to turn negative competition into positive competition on their own. Of course, they won't always be able to do it without your help and intervention, but I've had many parents tell me that the following three guidelines helped their children learn how to resolve conflicts and compete more positively. The next time your children start battling stop the game and:

- **Give your kids positive options for how they can react to a sibling's behavior.** Parents want their kids to take the "high road" when it comes to sibling rivalry, but many kids don't know what that means or how to do the more mature thing. Kids don't always know that they can disagree without fighting; they can walk away, offer to play again, play a different game, or ask for help in resolving their differences. You have to tell kids they have these options. Encourage them to use them on a regular basis.

- **Discuss positive options to resolve the conflict.** For kids who tease and torment each other after a victory or a loss you can institute the policy that, "After the game, shake hands and don't discuss it any longer." For siblings who fight while they play, try to generate ideas about how to continue playing in harmony. For example, you can suggest, "Once the game starts, you can't talk to each other" or "The first person to tease loses a point." When there's a disagreement, make them part of the solution. Ask them for some specific ways to resolve the disagreement, such as: "If the ball goes out this far, it's a foul. What other rules can we follow to help you girls play together?" Help them negotiate and make compromises, such as, "Judy agreed to give you the point, it seems only fair that you let her have the ball now."

- **Be clear about your expectations.** Let your children know you expect them to stick to the agreement or compromise. Tell them that you want them to resolve their problem but that you're available to offer additional support. "I expect you to follow the rules we agreed on. If you feel angry or frustrated you'll let the other know." Be clear about the consequences of not sticking to the agreement. "If you and Abigail continue to fight during badminton, then you'll be benched from playing this game together for the rest of the weekend."

With time, patience, and practice, a parent can help his or her children learn how to resolve conflicts and play well together.

60. Don't sacrifice one sibling's sports activities for another's

When one child's sport takes up a significant amount of family time, energy, and money his or her siblings usually suffer.

A family came to me for advice because they were told that their fourteen-year-old daughter Alyssa had "Olympic potential" in ice skating. These parents were caught in a dilemma that many parents face. On the one hand, they wanted to provide their daughter with all the opportunities to be the best that she could be. On the other hand, to be at the Olympic or professional level in ice skating or any sport requires an enormous amount of time and money. It also requires enormous sacrifice on the athlete's part and the family's part. It meant that the whole family frequently had to travel on the weekends to attend competitions around the state. The parents were unsure if they wanted to make this kind of investment but they wanted to do the right thing by their daughter.

They also came to me because the younger daughter, Sarah, was constantly fighting with her sister. In one of our first meetings, I asked Sarah how her weekend had been.

"Horrible," she said. "What do you think it's like for me to be dragged around every weekend from place to place watching her ice-skate?"

Sarah was bothered by the amount of time and attention Alyssa's skating competition sucked up and by the fact that she was expected to always tag along. I'm sure that Sarah's parents had no bad intentions but the message she was getting by being dragged from skating competition to skating competition was loud and clear: "Alyssa's skating career is more important than anything you want or need."

I don't blame Sarah for feeling upset and invisible. Maybe it would be obvious to you that Sarah's parents were making a mistake in terms of how they were handling Alyssa's skating. But remember, when you're in the middle of the situation, the solution isn't always so obvious.

We discussed new ways of handling Alyssa's skating. The family decided that only one parent would go with her to skating competitions while the other parent stayed with Sarah in order to give her an opportunity to develop her interests and athletic skills. If Sarah chose to come along to a skating competition then the entire family would willingly do so.

Parents need to make sure that they're paying enough attention to and not sacrificing the lives of the other siblings in order to pursue a scholarship, professional career, or Olympic path for one child. If there simply isn't enough money for all children to pursue athletic opportunities because one child's sport takes most of the financial resources, I would recommend downsizing her sport in order to allow the others to have opportunities. Remember, the chances of an athletic scholarship or an Olympic or professional career are quite slim. Equal opportunity in sports for siblings is the fairest way for parents to divide the family resources.

61. Encourage rival siblings to help each other in sports

I have seen remarkable transformations when rival siblings help each other in sports.

Keith and Jeremy, the battling siblings I mentioned earlier, could not play basketball with one another without it turning into a fight. The boys were both good athletes and both boys especially loved basketball. Keith was a great shooter and Jeremy was a great defensive guard. At my suggestion, their parents encouraged Keith to become Jeremy's shooting coach and Jeremy to teach Keith how to play defense.

This kind of helping can help bring up the good feelings that kids still have for each other. It worked for Jeremy and Keith. Though the boys still occasionally fought when competing in sports, they were able to get along much better and enjoyed playing basketball together against other kids in the neighborhood.

It's important to keep in mind that one of the core beliefs of rivaling siblings is, "I'm better [faster] [stronger] than Frank." When you encourage siblings to help each other build skills and practice together the belief can be transformed into: "I can run the fifty-yard dash faster than Frank but he can pole vault higher than me. We're both good at different things."

Basketball players Tom and Dick Van Arsdale are identical twins who played on the same high school and college basketball teams because they enjoyed it so much. Even at the professional level, the best moments of their careers, they are quoted as saying, were when they played together.

Tennis players Venus and Serena Williams have eloquently described the love and respect they have for one another as they both compete for the same tennis honors. From what I have seen and heard about these famous siblings, I suspect that the reason they are able to be so supportive of one another is because they see a victory for one as a victory for both. That comes, in part, from working together toward common goals and helping one another be the best she can be.

6**2**. Enforce the five rules of good sibling sportsmanship.

Good sportsmanship, specifically the way kids handle themselves before, during, and after competition, does not necessarily come naturally to children. You have to teach them how to be good sports in sports. Siblings who engage in negative competition can benefit greatly from learning five simple guidelines that promote positive competition. Teach your children to:

- **Agree on the rules of play.** Teaching or getting kids to agree to the rules of the game can save parents a lot of headaches. This is a big source of conflict for siblings—it often leads to the age-old lament, "Bobby cheated" or "Susan took my turn." Often, Bobby and Susan are playing by different rules. Make sure your children know what the rules are. Ask each of them, "Will you stick to these rules?" Don't let battling siblings engage in sports play until they both agree to follow the rules.

- **Be a gracious winner.** A good winner is a humble winner who does not use his or her accomplishments to make another sibling feel badly. Let your child know it's not okay behavior to taunt a sibling or gloat over a victory.

- **Be a good loser.** Tell your child that it's just as important to be a good loser as a good winner. A good loser does not make excuses or try to take away from the winner by saying, "I would have beat you but my leg hurts" or "You cheated." Let your child know that there's always a next time and another game to play. Remind him or her of past victories. This can help take the sting out of losing.

- **Don't engage in name-calling, teasing, or taunting before, during, or after play.** It can take a while for kids to break the habit of verbally abusing siblings, but it can be done. You have to make it clear to your children that as soon as either one calls the other a name or teases, the game is over. You may have to end a few games, but eventually most kids, once they know you're serious about enforcing this rule, will break the name-calling habit.

- **End the game appropriately.** Tell your kids to say, "Good game," to one another and show them how to shake hands. Then instruct them to move on to another activity without dwelling on the particulars of the game.

Teach kids the rules of good sportsmanship and frequently remind them of these rules. Over time, these new behaviors will stick. And don't forget to practice what you preach. Be a good model for your kids. If you're telling your child not to engage in name-calling with her sister but then you call your brother names during a horseshoe tournament or while playing backgammon, you will be sending a powerful and confusing message to your child about negative competition. Kids are profoundly influenced by what their parents do and how they handle themselves.

63. Honor individual differences in your children's sports abilities

Many parents make negative comparisons about their children's abilities. Sometimes they know they're doing it; sometimes not. Giving the benefit of the doubt, many of these parents simply don't realize how hurtful and damaging negative comparisons are to their children; otherwise I truly believe they wouldn't do it.

Rarely do you find siblings who have the exact same physical abilities. One may be talented in sports and one isn't. One runs fast and one has good eye-hand coordination. Pitting one's talents against the other is *not* a positive motivator for kids. I have heard parents ask their children questions like, "Why can't you catch more like your sister?" or "Jane isn't afraid of getting hit with the ball, why are you?" Making these kinds of negative comparisons isn't going to make Jessica a better softball player. It usually has the opposite affect. Jessica will probably miss more balls with the added stress of these unrealistic expectations. She and her sister probably won't be getting along well either.

It is important to be open and honest about differences in skill levels between children. Trust me, you might not like talking about the fact that Max can outrun his older brother or that Kimberly is a graceful gymnast and Sophie has two left feet, but kids are aware of differences in physical abilities. It's important for parents to take the lead in discussing these differences in a positive way. Be direct but nonjudgmental. You can say, "The reality is that Sophie can run faster than you can. I know that makes you feel bad sometimes but no two people have the same abilities in everything." Then help your child recognize that her sibling is not better in everything. "You're good at many different things too. Last week you won that tennis match and you won the spelling bee at school."

Honor individual differences in your children's sports abilities. Tune into and celebrate each child's uniqueness and never draw negative comparisons between your children's abilities.

VII

. . . .

INJURY:

Prepare your child, physically and emotionally, for her sport

Though sports can help kids stay healthy by keeping them physically fit, playing a sport also brings the risk of injury. Each year, the Centers for Disease Control and Prevention estimates that nearly a million children under the age of fifteen are treated in hospital emergency rooms for sports-related injuries. About two-thirds of sports injuries in children are sprains involving ligaments, which connect one bone to another, and strains involving muscles. While the majority of youth sports injuries are not serious, they can cause great inconvenience and emotional upheaval for both children and their parents during the healing process.

Many sports injuries can be prevented, however, when parents get involved and make sure their children wear protective gear, follow the rules of play, and are physically and emotionally prepared to play the sport.

64. Don't assume your child is safe because he doesn't play a contact sport or she wears her safety gear

It's almost hard to believe, but four out of five parents in a National Safe Kids Campaign survey said they believed that injury was "part of the game." More than half expressed little concern about the possibility of their child being hurt or injured during sports play.

I don't believe that these parents are uncaring. Usually, just the opposite is true. I believe the results of that survey indicate that most sports parents simply don't realize there are many active steps they can take to help keep their kids safe and injury-free. I also believe that until a child is injured, most sports parents don't realize the physical and emotional consequences that are involved in the healing process.

Many parents also don't believe their sports-playing children are even at risk. Though about 80 percent of all sports injuries are from playing contact sports like football, basketball, or soccer, your child can still become injured, even if he doesn't play a contact sport.

Rob was a Little League player who dislocated his shoulder while pitching. Samantha tripped during a volleyball game and tore the ligaments in her shin. Sean fell off his bike and broke his nose. Kelly fainted during a track meet from dehydration. These children were all injured playing noncontact sports. Sports parents always need to be aware of safety issues and the potential for injury, no matter what sport a child plays.

Following these nine guidelines will help keep your child safe:

- **Make sure your child wears all the required safety gear every time he plays and practices.** Know how the sports equipment should fit your child and how to use it. If you're not sure, ask the coach or a knowledgeable sports-equipment sales professional.

- **Warn your child about dangerous behaviors like steroid, diuretic, and laxative use for quick weight loss, and the risks of going overboard in weight training.** These can all cause potential injury and physical harm to your child. (For more information on steroid use and safe weight loss, see chapter 9, Self-Esteem.)

- **Set a good example.** If you play a sport, wear your safety gear too. Parents who ride bikes with helmets on are much more likely to pass this lifesaving habit on to their children.

- **Insist that your child warm up and stretch before and after play.** Many injuries occur in sports due to pulled muscles. When your child warms up and cools down, have her pay special attention to the muscles that will get the most use during play—for example a pitcher would warm up the shoulder and the arm and a soccer player would warm up her leg muscles.

- **Make sure first aid is available at all games and practices.**

- **Observe your child's coach on safety issues.** A safety-conscious coach will enforce all the rules of the game, encourage safe play, and understand the special injury risks that young players face.

- **Don't let your child play with or against kids who are significantly older or bigger.** Most teams are constructed of kids of the same age for a reason—it's safer. Kids about the same age usually weigh around the same and have roughly the same muscle development, strength, and skill level. If your child plays against an older child, he may face an opponent who is stronger and more coordinated, thus putting your child at a safety disadvantage.

- **Ensure proper hydration.** Dehydration is a serious medical condition. Insist your child drink at least two glasses of water before she even steps onto the field. In hot or humid weather, children of all ages should drink water every fifteen to twenty minutes while playing.

- **Take all injuries seriously.** Minor injuries can quickly become major ones if not treated properly. Always seek medical attention. Don't rush your child back to play until she is fully healed and her doctor gives the green light.

65. Do your homework if you're worried about injury

Parents want to protect their kids. Kids want to play sports, sometimes sports that, as parents, we don't approve of, like contact sports such as football and hockey, and action sports like skateboarding and competitive downhill bike racing, because we worry about injury. While I respect the right of parents to make decisions that they feel are in the best interest of their children, doing your homework can help you make that decision armed with the right kind of safety information. You want to find the best balance between being too restrictive of your child's activities and not restrictive enough.

Parents I know, for example, were against their twelve-year-old son skateboarding. After they researched the sport, however, they discovered that there are skate parks now with adult supervision and safety requirements, such as strict enforcement of knee, wrist, and ankle pads and helmets. The supervisor also provided training and lessons on how to fall correctly, which is an important consideration when evaluating an action sport. These parents decided that they would rather have their son skating in a supervised environment where safety was enforced rather than sneaking off on his own to ride his skateboard with his friends.

Having safety information will also help you explain to your child why you don't want him playing football or riding skateboards. Telling your child, "We don't want you skateboarding in the park; three boys received serious head injuries even though they were wearing helmets," is often more effective with getting kids to listen to you than saying, "Because we said so."

When my son Eli wanted to play football, my wife and I were worried. Though he's in great shape and has solid athletic ability in many sports, Eli is not a big kid. We feared that he would get tackled by bigger kids and get hurt.

Though our first impulse was to tell him, "No way!" we decided to check out the safety issues before making a decision. We talked to the coach. We talked to other parents. We asked about what first aid is available on the field and what procedures are followed in the case of an emergency. We looked at the safety guidelines and also observed several games to make sure they were enforced. We looked at the records the league kept on injuries. Because the team had a good safety record and weight limits and most of the boys were the same size as our son, we decided to let him try it out. We made an agreement that he could start practices and we would reevaluate along the way.

A dad whose daughter played soccer was worried that she would injure her nose or get a concussion by "heading the ball." After speaking with his daughter's pediatrician, and getting confirmation that heading the ball could cause injury, he decided that this move simply wasn't safe, and gave her a choice, stop heading the ball or leave the sport. His daughter chose to stay on the team.

Many action or extreme sports do encourage safety and mandate safety equipment. As I pointed out, there are now skate parks opening for kids to in-line skate or skateboard in a supervised environment. Do your homework before you announce that it's unsafe. You may ultimately determine that the activity is unsafe or too risky, but at least then you will be able to tell your son, "I saw two boys fall off their bikes and get injured despite the safety equipment they were wearing and I don't think it's safe" or "Dr. Jones gave me some statistics on head injuries among skateboarders and we feel it simply isn't safe." Kids are more likely to listen to you if you give them valid reasons rather than just forbidding it.

The Web sites of the National Athletic Trainers' Association (www.nata.org) and the National Youth Sports Safety Foundation (www.nyssf.org) are just two organizations that provide information about sports injury and safety advice for youth sports. Hockey, wrestling, football, gymnastics, and lacrosse—almost all organized youth sports—have national and local organizations that provide information about injury statistics and offer good safety advice. You can simply search the Internet or ask a coach for the name of an organization.

The bottom line on safety in sports is that you're the parent. You have the right to say no to your child. You have the right to refuse to endorse his involvement in a sport by not paying for equipment or driving him to practices. Though your child will be angry and resentful about your decision and may not understand the wisdom and caring behind it, you need to do what you feel is in the best interest for the safety and health of your young athlete.

66. Know the risks of too much sports play

Because of the trend toward specialized play in youth sports, overuse injuries such as tendonitis, bursitis, and chronic knee injury, are on the rise among children. Children are especially vulnerable to overuse injuries because their bones are growing.

Unlike acute injuries, like a blow to the head or a broken bone, overuse injuries are caused by an accumulation of repetitive mini traumas. Overuse injuries occur for a number of reasons: the pounding of the feet on a hard training surface, the throwing motion of an arm during baseball, the repeated motion of a swimmer's arm hitting the water at the same angle, the bending or twisting of the back in gymnastics, even improper footwear. Another common reason for a rise in overuse injuries among young athletes is a sudden increase in the intensity, duration, and frequency of training. Beth was a tennis player who practiced around twelve hours a week, then went to camp for the summer and played eight hours a day. She made it through about two weeks before her elbow became so painful that she had to leave the camp and take the rest of the summer off.

It used to be that only professional players suffered from overuse injuries, but now children as young as eight and nine routinely sustain these kinds of injuries. Children are especially vulnerable to overuse injuries because of the softness of their growing bones and the relative tightness of their ligaments and tendons during growth spurts.

Many young athletes are training like college or professional athletes; they practice for hours and do repetitive drills;

they play year-round and some are even on several teams during one season. Others go from one sport to another each season with virtually no rest or break.

We look at our kids and think, "He's so young" or "She's so strong," and we don't see their hidden vulnerabilities in the form of soft bones and tender cartilage. In order to protect your child from overuse injuries take these two important steps:

ONE: Be on the lookout for the typical pattern of symptoms accompanying an overuse injury.

First, a child heading for an overuse injury will experience sore muscles for a few hours *after* a workout, practice, or game. Next, the pain in the muscle or bone will persist *after* the workout into the following day. Then, the pain will begin *before* the end of the workout or game, and persist throughout. Finally, an overuse injury will settle in and the pain will persist with routine motions before, during, and after a workout, game, or practice.

If you see symptoms of an overuse injury, have your child evaluated by a doctor, preferably one with a specialization in pediatric sports medicine.

TWO: Set limits.

Parents have the final say in how much or how intensely a child plays. You may need to step in as Paul's dad did because the young baseball player was literally wearing his arm out from throwing too many pitches a week. "Paul will play baseball seven days a week, fifty two weeks a year," his dad told me. "He dreams of playing in the major leagues one day." Like many parents, Paul's dad worried about his health but also didn't want to keep the boy from pursuing his dream.

In the end, after consulting with a pediatric sports medicine physician, Paul's dad restricted the boy's playing time to three days a week and refused to let him go to baseball camp for fear that his arm would be permanently damaged.

Was Paul happy? Of course not. But sometimes as parents, we need to see the bigger picture for our kids. We need to make the tough decisions because our children simply aren't capable of doing it for themselves. (For more information about specialization in youth sports see chapter 4, Specialization.)

As a rule of thumb, kids need a day off from sports each week and a season off each year. Most kids can play every day for two or three weeks, but if a child is playing that intensely for a month or longer, she will wear out, both physically and mentally.

In the more serious cases, the overuse injury requires surgery. Some children can suffer for a lifetime from an injury that occurs during childhood, or the injury could cause osteoarthritis when he is older. But if your child suffers from an overuse injury know that in most cases, with physical therapy and adequate rest for the body and the mind, overuse injuries heal completely. When parents know what to look for and are willing to take the necessary actions to limit too much sports play, kids stay healthy.

67. Let your child know she should never play through her pain

Kids often get the idea from watching the pros and college-level players stay in the game with braces, bandages, limps, and expressions of agony, that you are supposed to rise to the occasion and play through your pain, no matter how bad you feel. Professional and college players often get a great deal of media attention and admiration when they manage to "do what it takes" to overcome injury and pain and win. Sports-playing kids know this and they will often try to apply the same standard to themselves.

Coaches sometimes encourage kids to play through their pain for the sake of the team or the tournament. I have also seen and heard parents encouraging their children to ignore their pain and play on. One dad whose son had a badly sprained arm yelled at him from the sidelines, "Shake it off! Be a man!" This was a ten-year old boy! Fortunately, the official and the coach forced the boy to stop playing.

You often see this "No pain, no gain" attitude in contact sports, such as football, hockey, and lacrosse. Football players will tell you, "If you're strong, you won't get hurt." This is nonsense; strength is not a safety precaution, yet many kids believe it is.

In professional hockey, it's practically a badge of honor to play with broken bones. Kids believe they prove their toughness by playing while in pain. They don't play with broken bones but they often brag to one another about their injuries and bruises. Injury is a part of the culture of the sport.

The rehabilitation process can become yet another arena

where unhealthy attitudes such as, "No pain, no gain," can cause your child harm. Yes, it's important to apply yourself to getting stronger and healing, but some kids will take it too far. They think, "If it hurts, it means I'm really pushing myself and I'll get better faster." Let your child know that pain in rehab is not the measure of improvement. Explain to him that he's setting himself up for a longer convalescence or a worse injury. Always encourage your child to follow the advice and instructions of any medical professional assisting him.

You can also encourage a healthy respect for her pain by doing the following:

- **Reinforce healthy attitudes by reminding her, "There's nothing noble or admirable about playing with pain."** Tell your child, "Don't ever play with pain just because you want your team to win" or "You're not a wimp if you stop playing, you're really smart." Kids who play contact sports especially need this reminder and they need to hear it often because they are more exposed to negative messages.

- **Help your child understand that pain is a signal from one's body that should never be ignored.** You do this by explaining, "Pain means that something is wrong and needs attention," and "I know that winning is important but it's not as important as keeping yourself safe and healthy." Explain that playing in pain can cause even more serious injury, sometimes long-term or permanent problems.

- **Give your child permission to remove himself from a game or a practice, no matter what his coach or teammates think or say.** Let your child know that when it comes to his body, he's the one in charge.

- **Explore your own attitudes about pain and sports injury.** If you become injured in sports play or while active, what do you tell yourself? If you tell yourself "Be a man" or "Just shake it off," it's likely that your child will pick up on this message and emulate you. If you are the kind of person who believes, "No pain, no gain," chances are your child will believe this as well. One dad told me that his daughter Maddie had "a high threshold for pain." I had to wonder if that was the reality given his competitive attitude about her sports career. It may have been that Maddie was trying to please her father by toughing it out when in pain or injured. It's important to remember that as parents we are the most powerful role models for shaping our children's attitudes about pain and sports play.

68. Teach your child how to articulate his pain

Kids often make general statements like, "My leg hurts" or "My arm is sore."

Moms and dads need to help their kids learn how to express their pain in more detail. Giving kids the means to express their pain is valuable for two reasons. First, it teaches them to understand the severity of their own pain. It helps them differentiate between minor injuries and major ones, an important skill for a young athlete. When a child knows that her pain is a signal that she's hurt, she can then take steps to protect herself, such as taking herself out of the game, not running so fast, or getting help from a coach. This can help prevent a minor injury from becoming a major one. Second, kids who can talk about their pain give parents more information so they can respond appropriately, such as keeping the child home from practice or taking him to a doctor.

The key to helping kids accurately articulate their pain lies in helping them develop a sense of its severity. You do this by helping them be more detailed and specific about where they hurt and how they feel. So when your nine-year-old child says, "My stomach hurts," you need to probe for more information, such as, "Well, is it a big hurt or a little hurt? Does it hurt so much that you feel like you can't breathe? Does it hurt when you run or walk?"

Here are two more suggestions for helping your child talk to you about his pain:

- **Use examples from your child's past experience.** Get your child to discuss her present experience by reminding her of a past one, such as: "Remember the time you slid into first base and sprained your knee? Does it feel sore like that or more like the bruise you got falling off your skateboard?" or "Remember how badly your tooth hurt and we had to rush you to Dr. Denton's office. Does the pain in your head bother you that much?"

- **Give your child a scale to use.** Establish a scale of one to ten. You say, "On a scale of one to ten, tell me how badly your leg hurts. One is it's kind of bugging me and ten is I'm having trouble walking" or "On a scale of one to ten, tell me how your stomach feels. One is you feel like you might throw up and ten is you can hardly breathe." In time, your child can tell you on her own, "When I slid into the base I hurt my elbow and it's a seven."

69. Determine if your child is trying to opt out of competition

Because young athletes often believe that "No one likes a quitter," children will sometimes fake an injury or develop physical ailments to avoid being judged by their teammates, coach, and parents. Some children will also pretend they are hurt if they worry that their parent will be upset if they want to opt out of a sport.

While I strongly advocate erring on the side of caution when a child has a physical complaint, sports parents do need to know that injury remains the socially acceptable way to opt out of competition. In my work as a sports camp consultant, I see this behavior quite frequently. One boy begged off to the infirmary complaining of a sore leg every time there was a high-pressure basketball game but the rest of the time he was fine and willing and able to play.

Your child may not consciously understand that she is making her leg hurt or creating that dizzy sensation in her head in order to avoid playing a sport. Kids do experience real physical symptoms from stress. While this is true for kids of all ages, children under the age of ten often don't know how to articulate a problem. They're more likely to tell you they're hurt in order to avoid playing sports.

If your child tells you he has an injury and you suspect that he's faking, take the following three steps:

- **Respond to the physical complaint.** Even if you suspect your child is faking an injury or illness, err on the side of caution until you have more definitive information. Keep her home or let her sit out and treat the symptoms accordingly. If your child seems to be in pain, seek medical attention immediately. If your child does not seem acutely injured or ill, but the symptoms persist, you should get a medical opinion.

- **Look for a pattern.** Does your child have a weak arm, a bruised knee, or a throbbing head when there's a play-off game or a particular game situation, such as bases loaded and he's up at bat? In similar pressure situations, such as the school spelling bee or a big math test, does your daughter complain of illness or injury? These are the kinds of patterns in behavior to consider, especially if there appears to be nothing medically wrong with your child.

- **Get your child talking about her experiences in sports.** If your child has gotten a clean bill of health, yet insists she's injured, there is something going on for her that's causing the behavior. The best way to help your child to open up is to let her know that it's safe to talk to you. You can say, "I believe that you think you're hurt and I'm concerned for you, but the doctor says you're fine. I'm wondering if there's something that's bothering you. Are you enjoying field hockey? Are you having a problem with one of your teammates?" or "Your leg seems fine when you're at home and at practices. But you feel pain when you're competing. It's okay to feel nervous. Are you feeling nervous when the game starts?"

Once you're able to uncover the real reason for your child's stress or unhappiness you can then help him deal with it. (See chapter 2, Competition, for strategies on dealing with competitive stress.) Though he believes that it's safer or more acceptable to be injured, you can help him understand that the truth is always better.

70. Be sensitive to the emotional aspects of healing

Parents often don't understand the feelings of loss associated with a sports injury. We look at our kids and think, "He'll be back in the game in three weeks or by next season, so it's not that big a deal." We assume, "She's young and strong, she'll heal quickly." Parents often don't realize that even when full recovery is possible, many athletes still feel a real sense of loss and sadness.

Evan was a twelve-year-old soccer player who had injured his knee during a game and couldn't finish the season. His parents didn't understand why he seemed so depressed; after all, they told me, he played for three quarters of the season and would play again next year.

But to Evan, soccer was a huge part of his life and his identity. He saw himself as a soccer player. Most of his friends were on the team or in the same league. To have soccer suddenly taken from him was a huge loss for the boy. His parents discovered that in order to help him heal they needed to be sensitive to the loss he experienced. They did this simply by acknowledging the loss. They told their son, "We know how important soccer is to you. We're so sorry you can't play right now."

Like Evan's parents, you can help your athlete heal from sports injury on an emotional level by taking these five steps:

- **Tell your child "It's okay to feel sad."** Let your child know that you understand what she's experiencing and that it's okay to feel sad; it's okay to grieve for lost playing time. You can offer support and reassurance simply by making a statement like, "Clare, I know how important swimming is to you. You must be feeling very sad that you can't compete right now." Validating your child's feelings will help those feelings of loss and sadness seems less scary and overwhelming.

- **Don't try to talk your child out of feeling sad.** It can be painful for a parent when a child feels depressed or sad, so our first impulse is to try to talk him out of how he feels. You don't want to say, "It's just a game" or "Come on, let me see you smile" without first acknowledging and permitting your child to have his feelings of loss. It's okay to remind your child of other hobbies, activities, or games he still enjoys. Tell him, "Just because you broke your arm, doesn't mean you'll never play again" and "After you give your ankle a rest, you'll be ready to play again in a few weeks."

- **Give your child as much medical information as possible.** When your child understands how she got injured and how she'll heal she'll feel more involved in her own recovery process. When kids feel involved in the medical process they feel less like victims and more empowered to heal and go on.

- **Encourage your boy or girl to channel her competitive feelings and energy into the rehabilitation process.** Some young athletes feel the loss of a sport because they miss the challenge and physical release. But physical therapy and rehabilitation can be challenging both physically and mentally. Let your child know he can use the rehab process to set and achieve goals, such as, "By next week, be able to lift twenty-five pounds with your knee" or "Let's see if you can walk a little farther today than you did yesterday."

- **Keep your child involved with the team.** Just because she can't play, doesn't mean she can't support her teammates. Encourage your child to attend practices, games, and team celebrations. If appropriate, ask the coach if she can help keep statistics. Part of the loss children feel when they are benched with an injury is missing the camaraderie and friendship of their teammates and the sense that they belong to a larger group.

71. Help your child trust her body again

Physically, Molly's elbow felt normal. After three months of rehab and rest, her doctor gave her the thumbs-up to play tennis again. But she told me she was afraid to serve because her elbow might "go out on me again."

When an athlete suffers an injury, she can feel betrayed by her own body. She may be afraid to play her sport again for fear of getting hurt again. Because of this fear, many injured kids avoid resuming play when they recover. Young people think things like, "I feel okay, but can I really trust my knee not to give out again?" This betrayal can be frightening for athletes of any age. Eight-year-old soccer players and twenty-eight-year-old football players alike can experience these kinds of fears associated with healing. Often the body heals before the mind. It's very normal for kids to be reluctant to return to play after an injury. But there are ways to help.

First, respect the fear. Don't push your child back into full, competitive play before she's ready. If you do, the stress alone can cause her to be more susceptible to reinjury. Give her time and reassurance that her body is strong until she feels comfortable again. Just because you would want to jump right back in and play, doesn't mean she is ready. There's absolutely nothing wrong or abnormal about a child recovering physically before she's recovered emotionally from a sports injury. Let her know it's perfectly normal to have fears about her body.

Second, help your child trust her body again and gradually get back in the game. You can do this by "working her up the ladder." Establish a four- or five-rung "ladder" that challenges her to gradually believe in her body again. Start from the physically and emotionally easiest and work toward the hardest. Molly's tennis ladder looked like this:

1. Hit forehand shots only.
2. Hit backhand shots.
3. Play a game with no serving involved.
4. Play a game with one or two serves.
5. Play a regular game.

If Molly's elbow started bothering her, her father would remind her to rub it and take it slow. He kept telling her, "It's okay to trust your body—ninety-nine out of a hundred times your body has come through for you."

Buck, a college freshman who injured his knee playing football, used this ladder to gradually trust his body again:

1. Jog in place.
2. Run in a straight line.
3. Run while cutting left and right.
4. Run and have someone bump you.
5. Play a game.

Don't put any expectations or time limits on how long your child stays at any one rung of the ladder. Don't rush your son or daughter. When she was ready to try serving, with encouragement and reassurance, Molly let her parents know she was ready. It's okay to ask and encourage her to play. It's okay to check in and ask, "How do you feel about trying the next step?" but let your child conquer her fear and build her trust back on her own timeline.

72. Respect the emotional effects of chronic injuries

An acute injury is one that a child will recover from, such as a sprain or a concussion. A chronic injury or physical condition is one that recurs, never completely heals, or one that will impact your child's ability to perform in sports for the rest of his sports career, such as asthma, arthritis, or an overuse injury.

Whether acute or chronic, all injured athletes are susceptible to feelings of loss and fear. Children who experience an acute injury such as a concussion or an ankle sprain can often channel their energies into the rehabilitation process. With help from Mom and Dad, these kids can get over their feelings of loss and fear and return to normal play.

But it isn't always so easy for kids who experience chronic injuries to keep a positive attitude. When you have a knee that will never be as good as new again, or a chronic physical condition such as asthma or arthritis, it's a challenge to channel your energies in a positive way. You can't say to a child with a chronic condition, "If you work really hard at physical therapy or do your exercises faithfully, you'll be completely fine one day." The reality is that some kids will work at physical therapy and they will get hurt again.

So while all kids who experience acute injury can feel sad and fearful, understand that kids with chronic injuries and physical conditions often experience these feelings on an even deeper and more significant level. The support and understanding you offer will be the same as for an acute injury but it will need to be ongoing and longer term.

Don't be surprised if you see your child go through various stages of grief as they experience the loss of their physical skill and ability, playing time, and identity. First they may be angry and say things like, "It's unfair, why did this happen to me?" They may go into denial and try to continue to play. They may try to bargain by saying things like, "If I can play one more game, I'll go to church every Sunday."

Be patient with your child. Kids with recurring or chronic conditions often feel frustrated. They think, "How can I go through rehab again? It's not fair that this keeps happening to me!" and "What guarantee do I have that I won't keep getting injured?" Rather than tell you what they're feeling, they act out in other ways, such as refusing to do chores or homework.

Though it can be frustrating for moms and dads to deal with a child with a chronic injury, know that how your child comes to handle a chronic condition has a lot to do with your attitude. If you act like it's the end of the world that your child has to quit the traveling soccer team because of arthritis in his knee, then he'll view it as a big catastrophe as well. But if you keep a positive attitude, chances are, he'll be positive too. Be a broken record with encouraging statements like, "I know it's hard, but it's not the end of the world" and "Even though you can't play football right now there are many sports which you can still enjoy. Let's talk about what you can try."

With your guidance, reassurance, and help, most kids eventually can reach a place of healthy acceptance about a chronic condition or injury.

73. Define the safe parameters of play for your injured child

Chances are, a child who loves sports will still want to play and participate despite a chronic injury or physical condition. Children with chronic issues are often able to continue to play sports in some capacity, usually by modifying their behavior or by changing sports. But parents often worry that the child will become further injured or debilitated.

Without a doubt, you need to seek guidance on whether or not your child can safely play sports from your child's doctor or physical therapist, and/or athletic trainer. I always listen to my children's medical specialists and take seriously what they tell me. When the issue is safety and your child's physical well-being, err on the side of caution.

If your medical experts give the green light for continued sports play, I recommend you do the following:

- **Make sure your child is present when you talk to his doctor or physical therapist.** He needs to hear from the professionals what he can and can't do to participate safely in sports. And he needs to clearly understand the physical consequences of violating those parameters. Tony, a squash player with a recurring knee injury, continued to run and cut as if his knee was 100 percent. He also had to be nagged and cajoled into doing his knee strengthening exercises. I suggested that his parents take him to the orthopedist for a more vivid reality check. After his doctor showed him the ten-inch needle they would have to use to drain his knee if it didn't heal on its own, Tony "got it." He finally took it easy on his knee and did his exercises faithfully.

- **Have frequent discussions with your child about the modifications she needs to make.** Children who are under the age of twelve need lots of repetition and reinforcement to change behavior. You usually can't tell a child, "No more sliding into bases," once or twice and expect them to remember not to slide. Much of their sports behavior is habit to them, so you need to frequently remind your child, "Remember, the doctor said you can't slide or jump for the rest of this season because if you do your leg might never heal." Ask your child to repeat back what you've said to make sure they've heard you.

- **Get your child to sign a contract with you.** Write down what your child can and cannot do in sports and then have her sign it. Let her know what can happen if she fails to keep up her agreement, such as, "We'll pull you off the team for the rest of the season if you continue to rush the net." Post the contract in a place where she will see it regularly, such as the refrigerator or closet door.

- **Talk to your child's coach.** Make sure he or she understands your child's physical limitations. Ask the coach to be your eyes and ears when you're not around.

- **Encourage your child to be open to trying new sports.** Gretchen was on the track team but her more frequent asthma attacks in the spring made it apparent that she couldn't continue running. After meeting with her doctor, it was decided that Gretchen would be better suited to playing golf in the fall and volleyball in the winter months. At first, Gretchen was reluctant to participate in these new sports, but after she tried them she discovered how much fun they were. If your child is unable to play a contact sport, encourage him to try a noncontact sport such as swimming, hiking, or bike riding. It can take several weeks or months before he or she adjusts, but most kids who are unable to continue in one sport do benefit from continued participation in another sport.

- **Reevaluate your child's condition periodically.** Chronic injuries can, if not heal over time, at least improve. In another six months your child may be able to play her sport again or be able to participate more fully in her sport. Again, you want to seek guidance from a medical professional. You also want to ensure that your child's continued participation in sports is not causing further injury.

VIII

QUITTING:

If it's not fun,
something is wrong

Your son has been on the wrestling team for three years and now suddenly, in mid-season, he wants to quit. Your daughter begged to quit track so she could join the swim team. You went to a lot of trouble to sign her up, bought her two expensive bathing suits, goggles, and a warm-up suit and now she says, "I don't like it."

Is it okay to let a kid quit a sport? Or does quitting send the wrong message about commitment and follow-through?

These are questions that have tied parents up in knots for as long as kids have been playing sports. You want your children to be happy, but you also want to teach them the values of follow-through and commitment. Each is important. So how do you know what to do?

Sometimes the right thing to do is to encourage a child to continue. Other times, just the opposite is true. You have to base your decision on your particular situation and child. But there are some guidelines that can help you make this important decision.

74. Let your child know that leaving the team is an option

Your child has probably heard "Quitters never win and winners never quit" and "Nobody likes a quitter" from the day he or she started playing sports. Many children today start playing organized sports at around age six. They are very young and likely to believe what they are told by their parents and coaches. They absorb these messages like sponges. Young athletes get these messages so often and so loudly from parents, coaches, and teammates that they can start playing a sport without realizing that there will be times when it's okay, and even appropriate, to "choose not to continue."

Though the intent behind telling kids, "Quitters never win," is positive—to spur kids on to success—the end result is often damaging. Kids believe that no matter how bad they feel playing a sport, or how much pressure they experience, they have no other choice but to stick it out. They worry that they are bad or inferior for not wanting to play. They fear that their parents will be disappointed in them for being a quitter.

Though adults know that if something isn't working, it's best to cut it short, kids, no matter what their age, don't necessarily know this. Kids need to hear from parents that messages like "Winners never quit" and "Nobody likes a quitter," though well meaning, aren't always the reality. Let your child know that there isn't anything wrong with her or that you're not disappointed with him if it doesn't work out in basketball. Comfort him with words like, "You're not a failure or a quitter if you've tried something and it didn't work out. Sometimes when we don't like or enjoy something, it's best to leave it behind. That's not the same as quitting because you don't feel like doing the work."

It's best to talk to your child about the appropriate reasons for choosing not to continue in a sport, preferably *before* the first practice starts. But it's never too late to sit down and have this important discussion.

If your child is between the ages of six and eleven, you should keep your words simple and general. Let them know that, "If you start T-ball and don't like it for any reason, you need to tell us about it. It may not be the best sport for you right now and that's okay" or "If you come home crying and upset we're going to have to talk about your staying on the soccer team. Fitting in with your teammates doesn't always happen right away."

Kids ages eleven and up can usually be told more explicit reasons when it's appropriate to stop a sport, such as if your child:

✓ Is being mistreated or abused by a coach or teammates

✓ Feels too much competitive stress or pressure to win

✓ Can't put in the time without having schoolwork suffer

✓ Feels embarrassed or shamed by his or her lack of skill

✓ Is injured or is in danger of injury

You can also let your child know the circumstances under which you would consider giving him your permission to stop playing, such as if your child:

✓ Practices hard but can't catch on to the game

✓ Isn't getting enough playing time

✓ Gives the sport his best shot, but simply doesn't enjoy the game

This is not to say that you will automatically give your permission for your child to stop, but rather, "If you find that you're not enjoying tennis we'll talk about what we should do" or "If for whatever reason you want to stop hockey, please come to us and talk about it."

When you give your children the option of stopping a sport, you help them see the bigger picture—everything they start in sports doesn't end up the way they wanted or wished it could be. Kids need to know that it's important to try new things but that they might not always work out, and that's okay.

75. Find the best sport to match your child's personality, interest, and talent

You can increase the chances that your children will want to continue to play sports and not drop out by helping them choose a sport that will be a good fit for them.

Children under the age of twelve especially need guidance when deciding upon a sport. You don't want to pigeonhole or force a child into trying a sport, but it's important to set kids up, especially kids who have previously had a bad experience, to have a good experience. The goal is for your child to feel competent and successful, not humiliated or overly frustrated. You certainly can't control everything; nor should you match your child with a sport that will be too easy and not challenging enough. You want your child to have fun, learn, and stretch out of her comfort zone. But putting a gregarious child who needs a lot of social stimulation into a more solitary sport like figure skating, may be setting that child up to have a bad or disappointing time. Likewise, an independent child may not enjoy being on the soccer team, where the play is very interdependent.

I advise you to consider three things when trying to help your child find a good sports match:

INTEREST. Some kids express obvious interest in a particular sport at an early age. From the time I was born, I always loved baseball. It was my favorite sport and it still is. But there are many children who love a variety of sports or aren't sure which they like. Many kids need to explore their options and this is perfectly natural and normal. When trying to assess your child's interest, answer these questions: What sport does your child seem excited about? What sport does she like to watch? What games does she enjoy playing with her friends? The answers will give you clues to assessing her interest.

SKILL. If the point of helping a child find a good fit in a sport is so that he can have a successful experience, then it's important to consider a child's natural abilities. Some kids can jump high and run fast and are natural track and basketball players. Others have flexibility and balance and are great ice skaters and gymnasts. I worked with a boy who had stamina and endurance but didn't like to run track. His parents encouraged him to join a cycling team and it was the perfect outlet for this boy's natural athletic abilities. Kids do acquire and hone athletic skills by playing sports, but in general, all kids have their strengths and aptitudes and it's helpful to play to them and not against them.

PERSONALITY. Certain sports lend themselves to a certain temperament. Parents know their own children. They know that Max gets easily frustrated when under pressure or that Sarah is highly competitive. Max might not enjoy tennis but Sarah might. A high-energy child who needs to run around would become frustrated by wrestling while a more aggressive child would do well. A shy child might prefer cross-country track over lacrosse. A sport like gymnastics is probably not the best choice for a child who is hard on himself or is a perfectionist.

When we help kids find the right sport in terms of interest, skill, and personality, we set them up to have a positive experience in sports. There's no guarantee your child will have a good experience but the right sport will dramatically increase the chances that he will want to continue to play.

76. Empower your child to deal with frustration

Frustration is a one of the biggest reasons why kids quit sports. Frustration is the reaction and internal feelings kids have when they can't do something correctly, like hit the baseball or intercept a pass. Kids often feel frustrated when they don't get what they want, like winning or getting another chance to play second base. Frustration is often the precursor to kids wanting to leave a sport. It's no fun to feel frustrated, so kids will often try to opt out to alleviate the unpleasant feeling.

But frustration comes with the territory. It's absolutely unavoidable. Sports are filled with unknowns and challenges. Things don't always go your way. You practice hard but still miss the ball. You play a great game but a teammate makes a big mistake. You're good but an opponent is simply better. All frustrating experiences, especially for a child.

Kids have varying levels of tolerance for frustration. There are some kids who frustrate easily. They want to quit whenever they feel frustrated. When kids have a low tolerance for sports being hard or for losing, they often become angry. This is why it's typical for frustrated kids to react by throwing equipment, and cursing, or with other inappropriate behavior.

For kids who are used to things coming easily, starting a new sport can be a big surprise. Suddenly, they've encountered an athletic endeavor that feels hard. Making mistakes and having a hard time catching on are unfamiliar and uncomfortable feelings for these kids and naturally they don't like it.

If your child no longer wants to play because she is frustrated, consider encouraging your child to hang in there and finish what's been started. This can be especially important for children who frustrate easily or experience frustration in many kinds of activities. Again, I don't advocate forcing a miserable child to play a sport, but always allowing a child to stop playing will not help her deal with frustration in the long run. Kids who never learn to handle frustration often leave sports. They don't reap the benefits that sports has to offer. They also feel bad about themselves. They think, "I can't do anything right" or "There must be something wrong with me."

If your child wants to quit out of frustration, take the following steps:

- **Help her name what she's really feeling.** If she says, "I'm bored" or "I'm sick of basketball," get her to talk about what she's really feeling. You can say, "It sounds to me like you're really frustrated because you want more playing time" or "What I'm hearing is that you want to shoot better in basketball but you don't feel like practice is helping. Are you feeling impatient to get better?" If she says, "I hate it" or "Coach is a jerk," tell her, "Wow, you seem really angry" or "It sounds like you're really upset with your coach." Putting the right name on what they're experiencing helps kids build self-awareness.

- **Tell him everyone feels frustrated sometimes.** Help your child understand that like the unpleasant feelings of competitive stress, feelings of frustration are unavoidable in sports. Frustration is not the enemy. Not being able to handle it is. As I've said before, when kids have unpleasant or scary feelings, it helps them to know that they're still normal.

- **Make sure your child isn't in over his head.** When they can't do something well or competently, kids feel frustrated. If your child wants to quit out of frustration ask yourself, "Is he in a league or on a team that he's not prepared for?" Some leagues or recreational teams are more competitive than others. If the other players are noticeably more competent, he may be playing on a level too high for his abilities at this time. With additional practice and time to develop his skills he will most likely catch up. He may need to play on a less competitive team for a while. A child who easily frustrates is probably going to have a harder time in spotlight sports like gymnastics and tennis, where he feels like his mistakes will be noticed on a much grander scale. It may be too much to ask of a child to expect him to thrive in certain sports. He may be better suited to soccer and hockey where the play is interdependent.

- **Get her to be specific about what help she needs.** Your daughter may tell you, "I suck at tennis and I don't want to play anymore." It is most likely that there are some aspects of the game she can do well. When kids are frustrated, they get so caught up in their anger and inner turmoil that they often see in black and white. They don't see their own gray areas and thus don't know how to ask for help. Get her to focus her efforts on figuring out where she needs help. You can say, "I saw you serve yesterday so I know you're good at that. Is it your backhand? Rushing the net? We can talk to Coach about getting you extra help on your backhand."

- **Give him permission to take a break.** Kids who get frustrated benefit by taking breaks from the activity. If your son is in practice, it's usually not a problem for him to say, "I need a minute." He can use that break to do some deep breathing and other calming techniques I discussed in chapter 2, Competition. One basketball player

I've worked with takes breaks when he's frustrated during practice. He runs around the entire court four or five times until he feels like he's burned off his frustration and anger. If your child becomes frustrated during a game, teach him to take mini breaks. For example, "When you're about to serve and you're getting frustrated, just stop what you're doing, take a deep breath, and count to five. As you're counting to five, repeat a mantra like, 'Easy does it,' 'This isn't a big deal,' or 'Try, try again.' "

Kids who persevere and learn to try and try again until they get it right learn how to manage frustration. They have better experiences in sports. They reap more of the benefits and rewards because they don't get fed up, lose hope, and stop playing. They learn to handle the ups and downs of sports. Helping your child deal with frustration in sports can be one of the most important actions a sports parent can take to ensure that their children will "stick with it" and "finish what they start."

77. Recognize that it's normal for kids to want to quit sports

If your child tells you that he or she wants to quit a sport, don't panic. Many parents tell me fears like, "Alison will never get into a good college without a sport" and "What's wrong with Joey? He can't finish anything he starts."

I promise you, just because your daughter wants to quit the swim team doesn't mean she won't get into a good college. Just because your son, at age eleven, can't stick to anything doesn't mean he'll never find a sport or hobby that he will stick to.

Moms and dads often blame themselves when a child wants to quit a sport. They worry, "I must be making mistakes if Henry always wants to quit whatever he starts" or "I'm not doing a good enough job." Though some parents are reluctant to admit it, they worry that there really *is* something wrong with Alison or that Joey does have some kind of character flaw.

In their panic, parents can forget that it's quite normal and even appropriate for kids not to want to continue a sport. Kids are young. They are inexperienced. They don't always have an easy time adapting to coaches or getting along with teammates. They don't always have the physical coordination to play a sport. Some kids become anxious or nervous when they're not good at something. Other kids don't get a lot of playing time and they lose interest sitting on the bench—can you blame them?

And sometimes, your child will give something a try and discover that he doesn't like it or thought it would be different. This is why kids try things out. They don't always know what they like and don't like.

Before the age of eleven or twelve, many children simply don't have the emotional maturity to know what it really means to make a commitment to something. They're just trying things out and moving along. This is normal "kid" behavior.

This is not to say that you should automatically let your child walk away from a sport or that you shouldn't be concerned if your child has a hard time finishing what he or she starts. There will be times when it's appropriate to give your permission to your children to stop playing and then other times when encouraging them to finish the season will be in their best interest.

The key is to approach your decision-making process without fear, panic, or anxiety. Don't think that if your child wants to quit softball or lacrosse he is doomed and will never finish anything. Tell yourself, "This is normal kid behavior and I don't want to turn it into something that's bad or undesirable. I will work with Derek and help him find the sport he can stick with."

I've worked with hundreds of children who seemed not to be able to stick to anything but were perfectly healthy and normal. With some parental guidance, these young athletes were able to find a sport and stick to it enthusiastically. Your child will, too.

78. Include your child in the decision-making process

Sam was a nine-year-old ice hockey player. Because Sam had expressed such enthusiasm and interest for the sport his father agreed to take him to 5 A.M. practices. Mid-season, Sam told his dad that he wanted to quit playing ice hockey. After a long argument his father finally "laid down the law" and said: *"You've got to finish what you start."*

Telling kids that "You've got to finish what you start," can lead them to feel guilty or bad about themselves. The implied message is that if you don't finish what you start there's something wrong with you or you're not good enough.

The other problem with telling a young athlete, "You've got to finish what you start," is that it isn't always true. It isn't always appropriate for a child to finish what he starts in sports or other things in his life. If your child was on a team with an abusive coach, you wouldn't want him to stick it out, would you? It's important to send the right kind of message to your child that he doesn't have a character flaw for wanting to opt out of a sport.

If you try to force a kid to continue playing a sport, you may be setting up a power struggle that can shut down communication with your child and disrupt your entire family. Kids over the age of twelve often rebel by not showing up for practices or not fully participating when they are there. Some kids will go along with your edict but they will act out in other ways, such as failing to do their homework, fighting with siblings, or talking back.

Instead of "laying down the law" include your child in the decision-making process. Engage him in a productive, open conversation about what he's experiencing in the sport. These four suggestions can help you get started:

- **Let her know that you will hear her out.** Reassure your child that you will consider what she tells you before making a decision. Many kids I work with tell me their parents don't really listen. As fourteen-year-old Mark put it, "My dad nods his head at me, but then he goes and does what he wants anyway." If your son feels like you've listened and considered his point of view, he is more likely to go along with your decision.

- **Be honest about your feelings.** Your child should consider your point of view too. You can say, "I'm surprised by this news" or "I'm shocked by what you're telling me because I thought you liked being on the swim team." These are honest statements but phrased in such a way that they won't cause your child to feel guilty about disappointing you or fearful about your reaction.

- **Establish a deadline.** Don't make a snap decision. Instead, give yourself time to think about it or to gather more information, but set a definitive date or time frame. If you want your child to continue for a few more games or weeks she will be more likely to go along if she understands there's a reason for it. You can say, "I'd like you to play until the end of the month. That way, I'll have some time to think about what you've told me and to discuss it with Mom and your coach."

- **Share your reasoning.** How many times have you heard yourself or another parent say, "Because I said so!" Yes, it's tempting to say this because you are the person in authority; however, letting kids know why you've made your decision can go a long way to keeping the peace. You show them that you considered their point of view, gave it a lot of thought, and have logic behind your decision.

79. Find out why he *really* wants to stop playing

Your child has a reason why she wants to quit the team. There may be more going on than simple disinterest or dislike. Though Abby says, "I'm sick of it," she's really intimidated by her tennis coach. Daniel tells you, "I don't like swimming anymore," but really a bigger boy on the team is bullying him. Depending upon your child's age, he or she could need help articulating the reason. Kids under the age of ten often need help naming what they are feeling. You may have to put words in their mouths, like "Do you feel uncomfortable [nervous/sad]?" Your older child might be reluctant to admit that he is nervous or uncomfortable or that she's not getting along with her coach or teammates.

Alex, a wide receiver on his high school's football team told his dad Stephen that he wanted to quit the team because he wasn't any good at football and his teammates made fun of him, "every day." Because Stephen worked at nights and on weekends, he wasn't able to attend many of the games. But he did know that his son was talented athletically and always had many friends. Something didn't seem right about Alex's reasons for wanting to quit. So Stephen made it a point to attend a few afternoon practices. While talking to the coach, Stephen found out that a few weeks earlier, during a close game, Alex had failed to catch a ball. The other boys called him "Butterfingers" in the locker room afterward. But as the coach put it, "He took it hard at first, but he seemed to get over it just fine."

Alex seemed fine on the outside, but on the inside, that mistake scarred him. Dropping what should have been an easy catch had shaken his confidence. Alex kept reliving the mistake in his mind and each time the mistake grew more horrible and embarrassing. He wasn't able to put the mistake behind him so he decided to try to escape the unpleasant feelings of embarrassment and self-doubt by quitting the sport he had always loved.

Alex had a common problem. Because they are working hard to be accepted and approved of by their parents, peers, and coaches, kids sometimes lose perspective in sports. Their identities are forming, they're vulnerable. They lack the experience to make sense of, or find meaning in, their bad experiences. Instead of "I'm learning," they think, "I stink." Mistakes become catastrophes, disappointments become unbearable, embarrassing moments become unforgettable. Rather than deal with these painful feelings, many kids will try to leave the team.

When you discuss your child's reasons for wanting to leave a sport or a team, you need to be aware that your child may not tell you the whole truth—not because she's consciously lying or he's trying to mislead you, but because a child's assessment and perception of the situation is not always accurate and because it can be colored by emotions such as embarrassment, jealousy, or fear. Your child may not know the real reason he or she wants to quit. So when she tells you why she wants to leave the swim team, you need to look for the "holes" in her story. Be alert for anything she says that doesn't ring true based upon your experience. For example, if your normally outgoing child who has lots of friends tells you, "None of the other kids on the team like me," I would consider that a red flag.

Before giving permission for their child to stop playing, Mom and Dad should consider doing some investigative work. Go to a few games or practices and observe your child as she plays and interacts with her coach and teammates. Speak to the coach and get his or her opinion. Speak to some other parents and find out what kind of experiences their children are having on the team. When you feel satisfied that your son's or daughter's perception of events or the situation is close to reality, then you will be in a better and more informed position to make a decision.

If you discover that your child has lost her perspective in sports because she made a mistake or she felt embarrassed, you should encourage her to "hang in there" and try to finish the season. As long as your child isn't in any kind of acute distress, such as not being able to eat or sleep, continuing is the best course of action. You don't want kids to quit because they've made a mistake or are embarrassed. That can send the message that "It's okay to quit if you make a mistake or feel uncomfortable."

Kids who want to quit sports out of embarrassment need help seeing the middle ground. When Toby would say, "But none of the other kids like me," his mom would give him a reality check and say, "That's not true. On Monday, I saw Cole joking around with you after the game and Harry invited you for ice cream." When you are consistent in reminding your child how things really are, they usually catch on.

80. Consider where your child is in the season

Though eight-year-old Madison had enthusiastically joined her soccer team, by mid-season she was complaining to her parents, "It's not fun anymore" and "I'm sick of it." By the end of the season, her parents had to drag her to games. "What should we do?" they asked me after a talk I had given to a parents' group. "We don't want to send her the message at such an early age that it's okay not to finish what she starts."

In this case, because it was near the end of the season and there were only three practices and two games left, I advised Madison's parents to encourage and support her in finishing the season. They told her, "We understand that you're tired of soccer but it's important to finish now that you're so close to the end. It's only a few more weeks and your team is counting on you to be there."

If your child has completed at least three quarters or almost a full season and is not in acute distress, such as not being able to eat or sleep, insist that she finish. It's important for kids to have closure with a sport. Finishing out the season lets them know that they did complete something. They can leave the sport knowing that it feels good to finish what you start even when reaching the finish line is a challenge.

If you're in the middle of the season and there are several games left, as long as your child isn't in acute distress, encourage him to hang in there and give it a few more weeks. It helps to establish a definitive timeline. Let your child know that during the next three weeks you'll be evaluating the situation and working with her in making the decision. You can say, "We'd like you to play at least until October before we decide" or

"Hang in there for three more games and then we'll talk about your not continuing." Kids are often more motivated to continue when there's an end in sight. Some parents find that when the deadline is reached, kids have had a change of heart. They are getting better through practice or have made friends on the team.

I don't think kids should be permitted to quit after the first or second practice or game. The problem with letting kids quit at the very beginning of a season is that many kids want to quit out of fear, frustration, or other reasons like feeling shy around their teammates. They haven't given the sport or themselves a chance.

Children can be hesitant, or even frightened, about trying new sports and interacting with new kids. This is true for kids of all ages, but especially true for kids in the six- to twelve-year-old range, who are just beginning to carve out their identities. As adults, we know that it usually takes some practice and trying before you're going to be good at an activity. We know that you often don't make friends with others right away but over time. Kids between six and twelve particularly lack this perspective. They can't do something and they immediately panic. One kid gives them the cold shoulder and they think, "No one likes me." It's therefore not unusual for a child to go to one practice or play one game and then want to quit because of this initial fear or uncomfortable feelings. This can be true even for kids who are really talented or who have a good amount of self-confidence in other situations.

Encourage her to stick with it for a few more practices or games. That way both you and your child will know that she gave it a legitimate try.

81. Give a fearful or anxious child extra support

If your child reacts to new situations with fear and anxiety, he will need extra support to hang in there and try to continue or finish the season. When a child is faced with the pressure of competition for the first time or has never learned to manage the feelings and sensations brought on by competition, he can become stressed out and fearful. Fear is a common reason why kids, especially under the age of twelve, want to quit sports, especially at the beginning of a season. It's important for parents to encourage kids experiencing fear and anxiety to stick with the sport. You want them to continue for at least a few games but be sure to provide extra help and support. The goal is to help your child get the experience of trying new things and managing, or overcoming, their fear.

I once heard a mom tell her son, "I don't know what your problem is, George. You're such a scaredy cat. None of the other kids are afraid of getting hit with the ball." Clearly, this mom was tired and frustrated. I've had those moments myself as a parent—you just want things to go smoothly and it's hard when your child isn't going along with you. However, these kinds of cajoling, belittling statements only make kids worry more and feel bad about themselves. They think, "There must be something wrong with me."

Instead, let a fearful child know that, "You can learn to manage and overcome your fear so that new things won't be so scary for you" or "We're going to help you feel more comfortable when you're playing tennis. Then, if you still don't like it, we'll talk about you not continuing." Teaching your child strategies to deal with the anxiety and stress of competition (see points 15 to 18 in chapter 2, Competition, and point 31 in chapter 3, Performance) and hearing encouraging messages can help your child be more receptive to continuing.

The following suggestions can help you support a fearful or anxious child:

- **Empathize with him.** Let your child know you understand what he's going through or that he's feeling badly. This isn't the same as giving in. It's saying, "I understand that you're feeling nervous and that's not easy, but it's important for you to give it another try."

- **Remind her of past success.** Point out situations—sports- or nonsports-related—where she felt nervous or anxious in the beginning but felt comfortable as she progressed. "Remember how nervous you were before you took the PSATs? You said after about twenty minutes you forgot all about being scared. So we know you *can* handle stressful situations."

- **Share an experience of your own.** Talk to your child about a situation—whether or not it was sports-related doesn't matter—in which you were afraid in the beginning but managed to end successfully. "When I had to get up and give a report at the last meeting, I thought everyone could hear my knees banging together. But I took some deep breaths and that helped me get started."

After giving it an honest try, be open to the fact that maybe your child is simply not suited to play this particular sport. It's not the end of the world. Rather than let your child go through several weeks or months of anxiety or misery, you should consider letting him stop. You want to be supportive and positive about this decision. Let your child know, "I'm so proud of you for hanging in there and trying hard for those last three games. Basketball just isn't your sport. That's fine. There is another sport out there that you'll enjoy and be good at. We'll help you find it."

If your child isn't emotionally ready to deal with the stress of competition then don't force it. This doesn't mean she will never overcome her fear. It simply means she needs more time or a different situation in which to overcome it. Keep supporting her in other activities. Encourage her to try new things.

82. Remember: If it's not fun, something is wrong

No child should be made to play a sport if he or she is miserable. If your child is coming home from practices and games the majority of the time in tears, with an upset stomach, unable to eat, or otherwise distraught, I would seriously consider giving your child permission to leave the sport or team. The point of youth sports is to teach kids lessons about teamwork, goal setting, and commitment, but it's supposed to be fun. If it's not fun, something is wrong!

When I met Aaron in my office, his face was red, wet, and swollen from crying. Before I could introduce myself, this twelve-year-old burst out saying, "I don't understand why my parents are doing this to me. Why are they making play baseball when I suck at it?"

Aaron had stuck it out and finished the season, which had been difficult, but now his parents wanted to sign him up again for the next season. This was truly a desperate and miserable boy. Frankly, after hearing Aaron's story, I didn't understand why his parents were making him play either, especially after he had given it his all for the last season.

When I talked to Aaron's parents, the reason eventually became clear. His dad, Stanley, told me, "Dr. Fish, I know that if my parents had made me stick to sports I would have felt better about myself. Instead they let me sign up for this and that and just drop out. It would have helped me if they had made me tow the line. I'm not making the same mistake with Aaron."

"No, you're not making the same mistake," I said. "But you are making another one. Aaron is truly miserable. What value, what lesson, do you think he can learn from this misery?

And," I added, "he stuck it out for the entire season, which took an enormous amount of effort and commitment on his part. That doesn't sound like a boy who is just signing up and quitting on a whim."

Unfortunately, I never saw this family again. Aaron's dad left my office, angry and disappointed because I didn't give him the green light on his behavior. I didn't tell him, "Way to go! Aaron will one day thank you for this." I told him just the opposite. I said, "I think Aaron may look back on this time and wonder if you really had his best interest at heart."

If you really want your child to continue playing and he or she is fighting it, you should do the following three things:

- **Be clear about your own motivations.** I hear parents say, "But Jane loves tennis!" and Jane is saying, "No, Mom. I hate it." Be sure that you're not ignoring the discomfort or pain that your child is experiencing because you are disappointed. Be sure that you don't have an emotional investment in your child's sport that is coloring your judgment, like Aaron's dad.

- **Understand what making a commitment means to a kid.** A six- to ten-year-old is capable of playing on a team and following directions, but before the age of eleven, kids usually lack the emotional maturity to understand what it really means to make a commitment to a team, a practice, a coach, or a season. You simply can't instill the values of follow-through and commitment through sports at this age. So if your child is truly miserable, is it worth it?

- **Get a second opinion.** Check in with another person who knows you and your child—your spouse, coach, relative, or another parent. Ask them to be honest with you about the situation. You can say, "Naomi wants to quit gymnastics, but we think she's just going through a phase and will be glad later that we pushed her to continue. What do you think? Do you think we're not seeing the whole picture?"

I've often wondered how Aaron managed with his unwanted baseball career. I suspect it hasn't gone well for him. I can only hope that his dad came to his senses and let Aaron stop playing. No child should be miserable in a sport and be forced to continue to play.

83. Reframe "quitting" as "choosing not to continue"

Nobody likes a quitter.

A "quitter" is someone who doesn't give it their all, someone who just gives up on a whim. No doubt about it, "quitter" in our achievement-oriented culture is an insult. That's why when your child wants to stop playing a sport, you want to be careful not to label him or her as a "quitter." You should be careful not to communicate to your child that she "can't stick to anything" or that he's "the one child in the family who doesn't finish what he starts."

When a young identity is forming, it can be damaging for a child to get the message, *"You're a quitter."* A child can feel bad about herself, or feel guilty because she thinks she let you down. And the label could stick to the child for years to come. She may grow up believing, "Well, I don't finish what I start, so why start anything?" She may think, "I'll never be a winner because I'm just not made for it."

"Choosing not to continue" is a much more positive term than "quitting." There's no negative connotation to "choosing not to do something" nor should there be! Your child gave soccer his best shot or he may have tried really hard in field hockey but it simply didn't work out. So if you decide that the appropriate course of action is to give your child permission to stop playing, why call it or think of it as quitting if that puts a negative spin on it?

When you reframe "quitting" as "choosing not to continue," you take any stigma out of leaving the sport for children. If you decide to give your permission and let your child stop playing, a positive attitude will help your child to move on and find a new sport without the pressure or fear that he or she has a problem or can't do something right.

Wanting to stop playing a sport may indeed be a phase; it may be that your child truly is having a bad experience with a sport. Either way, "choosing not to continue" is a much more positive and empowering word choice than "quitter."

84. Show your child the right way to leave the team

One of the boys on my son's baseball team just stopped show-ing up one day, the day before a game. He was the shortstop, a key position on the team. The coach called his parents and was told, "We've decided that he's not going to play anymore."

I don't think it's ever appropriate for a child to simply not show up if he or she is leaving a team. Because it isn't always easy to face the coach and say, "I'm not playing anymore," par-ents often allow their child to not show up. This is a mistake. If you're telling your child it's okay not to continue, which it often is, why let it seem like they're simply slinking away or sneaking off? You create an awkward situation later if his coach or team-mates are people he will encounter again.

Think of notifying the coach of your decision as an oppor-tunity to teach your child a lesson in follow-through, responsi-bility, and respect for others. You should probably accompany your child if he is under the age of twelve as he may feel intimi-dated dealing with an authority figure. You can also do this by phone with your child on the extension. Teach your child to say, "I've decided not to play anymore. I want to thank you for the time you spent with me. Good luck with the rest of your season."

If it was an uncomfortable situation that your child is leav-ing—because she didn't like the way coach treated her or the coach's overall style, take the lead with the coach and say some-thing like, "Beth won't be playing volleyball anymore. It's not in her best interest to play." If you get an argument from the coach, or he or she tries to talk you out of your decision, be polite, calm, and assertive. Simply stick to your line: "We feel it's not in Beth's best interest to play, but thank you for your time."

When your child leaves the team with dignity and shows respect for his coach and teammates he has closure on the experience. It's important for kids to be able to walk away from the particular sport or team with a positive feeling, a feeling of, "Well, it didn't work out this time, but I did learn some things and I'm glad I tried." A child who simply fails to show up may feel positive in some ways but may also feel bad about the way he left.

IX

· · · · · · · · · · · ·

SELF-ESTEEM:

Empower your child through sports

Self-esteem is how we think and feel about ourselves. It encompasses our confidence levels (how competent we feel), our identity (who we think we are in the world), and our body and self-image (how we see ourselves).

Sports are a great place for kids to feel good about themselves and increase their self-esteem. When kids are taught athletic skills and are able to perform them competently, their self-esteem is bolstered. The acceptance and belonging that kids experience by playing on a team is another contributor to healthy self-esteem. When young athletes feel good about themselves, they are less likely to use drugs and alcohol and more likely to graduate from high school and college.

But there are no guarantees. There are plenty of kids playing sports with low self-esteem, even athletically talented kids. Adolescence, a critical time of identity development, is a time when many kids' interests change. Kids become self-conscious in a new way. They're under a lot of pressure to fit in and to look attractive. For some, interest in sports or their commitment level to sports changes. Coaches, teammates, and the league in which your boy or girl plays also contribute to your child's feelings of self-esteem. Fortunately, parents play the largest role in ensuring that sports has a positive impact on their children's self-esteem, even if they decide to alter or lessen their participation.

85. Challenge the high value that our society puts on sports

There's no question, our society values sports. The world of sports receives far more attention now than in recent years. Back in the 1960s and 1970s, social issues like the Vietnam War, civil rights, and the women's movement captivated everyone's attention. Now, it's the Super Bowl and the NBA Playoffs. Cable and satellite TV have certainly brought more kinds of sports, more often, into our family rooms. Remember when it used to be Monday Night Football and Sunday golf tournaments and that was about it? Now, ESPN plays twenty-four-hours a day, seven days a week.

There is something about star athletes that captivates everyone around the globe, but Americans seem particularly affected by sports and its heroes. Americans especially value physical fitness and physical strength. Perhaps this is a natural by-product of a society with a high standard of living—we spend more time devoted to our pastimes and hobbies.

From this increased attention on sports and sports figures, kids get the message: To be successful in our society you need to be athletic. To fit in, you need to play sports. Fitting in athletically to meet our culture's definition of success is yet another source of pressure for young athletes, especially from the ages twelve and up, when kids start looking more to their peers for approval and acceptance. Not being athletic in a culture that so values athleticism can be devastating to a child's self-esteem and identity.

Here are four ways you can help your child counter the negative cultural pressures to be athletic:

- **Accept your child, no matter what her athletic skills are.** When a child truly feels accepted by her parents—when she believes, "Mom and Dad still think I'm number one, even when I drop the ball or run slowly"—she will feel less pressure to fit in athletically in the eyes of her peers, coaches, and society at large. It's easy to help your child feel accepted—simply provide verbal reassurances like, "I know you'd like to be a better hitter, but we're so proud of you for trying hard. That's the most important thing to us." Avoid criticizing your youngster for not being athletic enough. When you criticize you send a message that you don't accept your child. I was shocked to hear a father tell his son, "Come on, you're never going to make the team if you run like a girl!" I'm sure he didn't mean to be cruel, but children are crushed when they think that their parents want them to be more or different than they are. I'm sure this dad thought with a bit of cajoling his son might run faster. But he was wrong. What this dad should have been saying (in private) was something more supportive like, "I know you can't run as fast as a lot of the boys in your class, but you're still young, your body is still developing. You need to give yourself some more time. Look at how good you are at art. You've been doing that so well since you could hold a pencil." By pointing out what your child does well, you can take the pressure off to be athletic.

- **Appreciate all of your child's accomplishments.** I get excited when my daughter Talia makes a goal in soccer. I'll give her a hug and say, "Great job!" But I try to get just as excited when she comes home with an "A" on a math test or a ribbon for making second place in a spelling competition. I'll give her a hug and say, "Great job!" for those accomplishments too. When I recognize her sports and nonsports accomplishments equally, she understands that she doesn't necessarily have to be a good athlete to get my attention.

- **Expose your child to accomplished professionals in other fields.** At least once or twice a month, turn off the sports channel and turn on a documentary about an explorer, famous artist, or musician. Tell your child that even though these interesting people don't get as much media exposure as do the big-time athletes, their contributions to society are significant and valuable. Talk about ways you can be a valuable and contributing member of society outside of sports. You can remind kids that sure it's great to hit a home run or score in soccer but that volunteering at a nursing home or helping a friend or neighbor are worthwhile activities too. And if they see you doing these things too, such conversations will be even more effective.

- **Talk to your child about the realities of making a professional team.** Because they see the pros so much on TV kids can get the idea that you have to play on that level to be accepted and admired. Let them know that very few people "make it" in sports and that the ones who do sacrifice a lot of other things like time for education, art, and music to get and stay there. Kids need to understand that though they see the professionals in the media, most people who play sports, even very talented players, never appear on TV or get written up in the newspaper.

When children see who they are and understand how they fit in both inside *and* outside of sports, you empower them to become well-rounded people with confidence in more than one area of their lives. They can get their self-esteem and identity from a variety of sources. They can discover all of their passions and interests and not only their athletic ones. You also empower them to perform well in sports. As I discussed in the chapters on Quitting (chapter 8) and Specialization (chapter 4), kids who are under too much pressure in sports and kids who believe their acceptance is based upon sports performance often burn out or lose interest in sports. Kids who have a balanced attitude about winning and kids who are allowed to explore other interests are often the ones who have healthy levels of self-esteem. They are able to stick to sports through high school and beyond.

86. Support trophy-giving for young athletes

It is common practice in most youth and recreational leagues, summer camps, and in some elementary schools, to reward all kids with trophies and/or plaques at the end of a season. Many parents, coaches, and youth sport officials believe that if a child under the age of ten starts and finishes a season, he should be rewarded with positive reinforcement for his participation. Plus, young kids love getting trophies and plaques. I see how excited my twins, Ari and Talia, get when they receive an award at the end of their soccer league. It makes them feel good about themselves.

But there is an increasingly popular school of thought that says if one of the goals of youth sports is to help young kids feel good about themselves, they need to develop an internal reward system based on effort and not one that is dependent upon external rewards like trophies. Self-esteem development should be internally rather than externally driven. We don't want kids to expect and want the reward for sports participation; we want them to participate for other less tangible, yet rewarding reasons, like effort, fun, and commitment.

I agree that if an athlete is too focused on external rewards, whether it's a sixteen-year-old who plays only to get a trophy or a professional football player who plays only because he's well paid, he or she may not develop an internal love and appreciation for a sport. When there's no internal payoff to playing sports, athletes will quit when the external rewards cease.

But I disagree that giving young athletes trophies sets them on a negative path too dependent on external rewards. I believe that if an athlete twelve-years-old or under finishes what he starts in sports, a tangible reward like a trophy or a plaque, in addition to verbal praise, is helpful to his self-esteem development. Your child can hang a plaque on the wall or place a trophy on the mantel or shelf. She can see it and be reminded of her accomplishment. It's tangible evidence of her experience and she can be proud of that. At this age, young athletes are not as able to feel pride purely based on accomplishment and effort. External rewards help trigger positive internal feelings.

Of course, kids who get trophies need Mom and Dad to provide those reminders of all the reasons to play sports (see point number 3), that winning and trophies aren't everything in sports. A child also needs honest feedback to help him assess how he's really doing. When your child says, "I stunk today," you need to be there to provide the reality check. You don't want to be dishonest and say, "No, you were fabulous," because you think that will help him feel better about himself. That usually backfires. Kids know whether or not they got to base or crossed a finish line. You can't pretend. It sends the wrong message: "Deny what you don't do well." That attitude is not conducive to positive self-esteem development. If your child didn't play well you want to acknowledge that but provide the whole picture: "Well, you didn't get a hit in T-ball today, but you did get a hit just last week. I bet if you keep practicing you'll get more hits. And you made that great catch in the second inning. Some games you get a hit and some you don't. That's how it works in all of sports."

Once kids are entering the middle school years, around the sixth grade, they are more able to understand that the trophies in sports don't go to everyone anymore, they go to the kids who've accomplished more or the team who wins the championship. Twelve-year-olds are more capable of developing an internal sense of pride based upon their efforts and accomplishments. If Mom and Dad have been, and continue to be, consistent in providing honest, helpful feedback and the reminders of all the reasons to play sports, kids won't need or depend upon trophies and plaques to trigger positive internal feelings—they will be able to do this on their own.

87. Help your child develop a positive body image

If you've seen a modern version of G.I. Joe or other action figure dolls recently, with their wide chests and muscular arms, you would better understand the body-image pressure facing boys today: In order to be considered attractive you need to have muscles.

Body-image related disorders, long thought to be only a girl's problem, are on the rise among boys. Specifically, muscle dysmorphic disorder, thinking their muscles aren't big enough, is a serious problem for many young male athletes today. Poor or distorted body image in boys fuels unhealthy behaviors like steroid use and compulsive weight conditioning.

Girls are also falling prey to muscle madness. It used to be that fashion models and actresses had only to be thin to be considered desirable and attractive. Now, it's super-thin *and* super-conditioned, like Jennifer Aniston and Courteney Cox, two popular TV stars.

Poor or distorted body image in girls can fuel unhealthy behaviors like overtraining and unhealthy dietary habits, such as eating only one meal per day, which can lead to serious nutritional deficiencies. Fortunately for girls, there are popular female athletes who have become more visible in the media, like three-time WNBA All-Star Katie Smith and soccer star Mia Hamm, who are not extremely thin but are in good overall physical condition. These women represent a more realistic and healthier athletic image for girls.

One of the biggest issues for parents with young athletes is helping them feel good about their bodies, despite a cultural pressure to be muscular and lean. Here are four positive ways you can do this:

- **Raise your child's awareness about media messages versus the real world.** Teach your child to view advertising, fashion magazines, sports and entertainment programming, critically. Help your daughter cultivate an awareness that she's being assaulted with a variety of messages about how she should look or what is considered attractive. Let your son know that the action heroes in movies do not represent what most men look like. Teach your kids to talk back to these messages. Challenge them to think proactive statements like, "No, I don't have to look like Jennifer Aniston on 'Friends' in order to be pretty. Very few women do look like she does" and "The guys in this body-building magazine spend a lot of time working to look like this. They also are airbrushed and shown in the best possible light." One mom took her teenage daughter to the mall and sat down by the fountain. She challenged her to find two adult women who had lean and conditioned bodies like the woman in a print ad for a pair of jeans her daughter wanted. They sat there for an hour and didn't find one woman who could have fit into the jeans.

- **Talk to your child about what his athletic body can do.** Kids with body-image problems tend to focus on what's wrong rather than on what's right. Remind your child of his physical strengths as an athlete on a regular basis. You can say, "Your legs aren't big; they're healthy, active, and strong. It's wonderful that you have legs that can carry you on a five-mile run. And look at Anna Kournikova and Mia Hamm. Their athletic bodies are considered very attractive." Encourage your son to think about how strong and vital he feels when he plays sports by asking questions like, "How does it feel to run a mile?" or "Did you notice how long you were running without getting tired?"

- **Be cautious with criticism.** When many parents offer what they consider to be helpful advice, "If you think you're fat, you shouldn't be eating French fries," or "Those jeans are too tight. They make your backside look huge," kids hear criticism. Children are very susceptible to negative body-image messages from parents. If kids don't feel, "Mom and Dad think I'm attractive," they're not going to feel confident about their looks in the outside world. When kids are ages twelve to seventeen, the period of identity development, they are particularly vulnerable and sensitive to being criticized or embarrassed in front of their peers. If you have any feedback for your children about how they look, give it to them in private.

- **Find out what your child is thinking.** You can't fight an enemy you don't know. Ask your son or daughter, "How do you see yourself?" "When you look in the mirror, what do you see?" and "How do you define attractiveness?" Knowing his attitudes and self-perceptions will help you reinforce the positive ones and change the ones that hurt, like "Girls only like guys with big muscles." You will have the opportunity to start a dialogue about how you define attractiveness and how society may define it. You can say, for example, "Most guys *think* that girls want big muscles. But what girls really like is a boy who treats them well and has a good sense of humor."

88. Be extra supportive during puberty

Since he was ten years old, Tony dreamed of playing football for Penn State. The reality is that now that he's seventeen, he's just not big enough. Though he can play on the high school level, and he's good, he would get crushed in college.

Jamie could run like the wind up until the age of fourteen. After that, her body changed and developed. She simply wasn't as fast anymore. Though she could still run faster than average, she would never achieve star status again. She ended up leaving the track team.

Adolescence can make young athletes feel like strangers in their own skin. Kids who didn't give all that much thought to appearance can become obsessed when puberty hits. I've seen boys grow so quickly at fourteen and fifteen that they literally trip over their own feet. My neighbor's son was a good basketball player until he hit puberty. Suddenly the boy was uncoordinated, as if his arms and legs were too long for his body. I assured his dad that his son needed some time to grow into his new shape. It's common for kids to become awkward in sports during the adjustment. A friend's twelve-year-old daughter quit sports because her breasts developed before the other girls on her lacrosse team and she felt self-conscious. These are the painful realities of adolescence that kids who play sports need help dealing with.

Kids always need the support and encouragement of their parents, but puberty is an especially critical time for young athletes. This is the age where kids are more aware of their peers and they crave social acceptance. Yet, it's also the time when they become most unsure of themselves, how they look, and how they fit in.

Here are four things you can do to help your son or daughter successfully deal with a changing body and body image:

- **Prepare your child in advance.** When your boy or girl is prepubescent (approximately eleven for girls and twelve for boys) discuss the physical changes he or she can expect to experience and how that might affect your child's ability or desire to play sports. Reassure your youngster that he or she will adjust with supportive statements like, "It's not easy to have your body change into something unfamiliar, but in time, you are going to feel much more comfortable. You may not be able to run as fast for a while as your legs fill out or you may decide to try something new. Either way, we'll be there for you."

- **Don't make any promises.** I knew a dad who kept telling his son that one day he would be as tall (over six feet) as he was. Guess what? The boy was five feet seven inches. Genetics is no guarantee that your child will be short or tall. Most boys would rather be tall than short and muscular than thin. Most girls would rather be average height than tall, and thin rather than stocky. But you don't know how a boy's or girl's figure is going to turn out, so don't make assurances. You can be optimistic but be realistic too. You can say, "Most of the boys in our family are tall, but a few are average height and they've all done well in sports too" or "It's true that most of the girls in our family developed breasts after the age of thirteen, but that doesn't mean this will be true for you. There's a wide range of normal."

- **Validate her loss.** Don't gloss over your child's experience; this will make her feel worse. Jamie's mom: *"After Jamie's body changed and developed, she couldn't run as fast. She decided to leave the track team. I asked her how she felt about leaving the track team. She told me she felt confused and sad. I told her that I didn't blame her; it was a big loss. The track team was a big part of her life and identity. She had many friends on the team. Being good at track gave her validation and confidence. I reminded her that becoming a woman is an exciting experience and that she will get used to and love her new body in time. We talked about what other sports she might feel comfortable playing. She's not sure right now but we're going to help her explore some options."*

- **Honor his feelings about his body.** He may think he's a "shrimp" and she may think her hips are "way too big." You may not agree with the evaluation, but don't deny your children's perceptions, you may only alienate them. Respect the way they see themselves but let them know you don't see them that way. Challenge them about the way they see themselves and what they think is attractive. For example, you can say, "It must be hard to feel short compared to so many of the other boys. But look how strong you are. Being tall doesn't guarantee you happiness or popularity—but having a great personality and treating everyone with kindness is a good start." Continue to provide positive messages to your daughter. Tell her, "There is no one standard to measure physical beauty. The models that you see in magazines aren't reflective of most women." Provide her the reassurance that no matter what her size or weight, "I love you just the way you are." Over time, these positive statements can help to raise your child's awareness about her body image and help her to see herself in a more favorable and realistic way.

89. Educate yourself about the dangers of eating disorders

As a young child, Naomi seemed so confident, even carefree. She's played lacrosse and field hockey since she was eight. She's always had a strong body and she seemed so proud of herself. We just didn't think she would ever be at risk for an eating disorder like anorexia as a teenager. She's down to 100 pounds and may have to be hospitalized.

Barry became obsessed with his weight when he made the varsity wrestling team. He would have exercised morning, noon, and night if we'd let him. We didn't think that boys suffered from eating disorders. We thought he would get over it. He's now in college and still battling bulimia.

Sports can do a lot for kids by increasing self-esteem and therefore steering them away from dangerous behaviors such as smoking and drinking. But what sports *can't* do is prevent a girl or a boy with low self-esteem from developing an eating disorder. In fact, athletic involvement can make an eating disorder even harder for parents to spot. Strict dieting and vigorous exercise, two of the red flags of eating disorders, are often expected and accepted behaviors in sports.

Though usually considered a girl's-only issue, eating disorders afflict boys as well. It's estimated that 90 to 95 percent of eating disorders among athletes occur among girls, but that still leaves a large number of boys at risk. Male athletes are especially at risk for developing an eating disorder in sports that require lean body mass or where players compete in weight classes like youth football, body-building, and wrestling. A high school wrestler I know would work out in a rubber suit in a hot room to lose weight quickly—a very dangerous practice that many wrestlers and body-builders employ.

Some sports, such as gymnastics, ice skating, swimming, diving, wrestling, rowing, and dance may promote unhealthy attitudes about eating and body image in females and males by valuing and rewarding a lean body type. Low body fat and low weight are considered essential for top performance in these sports. As a result, young athletes can be driven to dangerous behaviors such as using steam baths to lose weight, starvation, and binging and purging in order to meet the ideal. They may come to believe that the only way to compete and excel in the sport is to be thin.

Boys and girls who play other sports, such as soccer, lacrosse, basketball, and track, swimming, and softball may believe that if they weigh less, they'll be faster and able to play better.

For girls especially, there's the societal pressure to be thin. Even though having an athletic body is now desirable and accepted as attractive, thin is still "in" in our culture. Athleticism, with its emphasis on muscle development and strength, is sometimes in conflict with the image many girl athletes have of the ideal body being thin and small.

The pressure of competition and the desire to win are other important factors in developing an eating disorder. An athlete may restrict his eating before a competition because he believes that he will be lighter and faster and therefore more likely to win. The pressure of competition—when it's too high—causes many kids to experience anxiety and depression. Some react by using food as a means of control. They think, "I can't control whether or not I'm going to win, but I can control how many calories I allow myself to eat."

Every parent of a young athlete twelve years old and up

needs to have his or her antennae up about eating disorders, specifically anorexia and bulimia. Anorexia is self-starvation. An anorexic will persistently and regularly deny herself food, despite being hungry, weak, and malnourished. I wouldn't panic if your daughter forgoes a meal once in a while because she's late or doesn't feel well, but I would certainly pay attention if she's skipping meals on a regular basis.

Bulimia is often referred to as "binge eating." Young people with bulimia will eat excessive amounts of food in a short period of time and then purge it from their systems, most commonly by vomiting or using laxatives. Of course, every teenager will "pig out" now and then on pizza, ice cream, and other junk foods. As long as it's occasional behavior, I wouldn't worry about it. Bulimia, on the other hand, is characterized by a pattern of binge eating, whether that be once a day, several times a week, or every time before a big competition.

Here are steps you can take to educate yourself about this critical issue:

- Talk to your child's doctor about what your son's or daughter's healthy weight should be, based on age, height, and body type. Make sure your child falls within the healthy limits as he or she ages.

- Read literature from the library and the Internet about eating disorders so you will know the signs, symptoms, and what you can do to help your son or daughter if an eating disorder develops. The signs and symptoms are similar for boys and girls.

Your child may be at risk for anorexia if he or she:

✓ Talks or worries about weight on a regular basis.

✓ Restricts eating. A child will regularly skip meals or eat only a small portion of his or her meals.

✓ Compulsively exercises above and beyond the demands of normal training.

✓ Experiences a dramatic weight loss within a month or a six-week period.

✓ Has a distorted body image. She may insist that her legs are huge when they aren't. He may see himself as being heavy or fat when he's normal or underweight.

✓ Becomes preoccupied with the calories or fat in foods.

✓ Loses her menstrual period. Girls who are significantly underweight will no longer get a period.

✓ Wears baggy clothes. He may be trying to hide his body because he is ashamed of it or she may be trying to hide her thinness.

✓ Grows fine hair on her face and arms, which indicates the body is trying to compensate for a lack of adequate fat. Our bodies need fat for warmth.

Your child may be at risk for bulimia if he or she:

✓ Shows compulsive concern for her weight and shape.

✓ Compulsively exercises or conditions above and beyond the demands of normal training.

✓ Uses drastic measures like steam baths, laxatives, and rubber suits to lose weight.

✓ Acts secretively about food and food consumption.

✓ Spends time in the bathroom after meals. A child may run the water in the sink or bathtub to hide the sounds of vomiting.

✓ Is weak or confused. May be signs of dehydration from vomiting.

- Look for patterns in your child's eating habits relating to competition. Notice if your daughter eats more or less before competition. If so, your child may be using food as a way to deal with her emotions around competition. Talk to her about the importance of eating healthfully, especially before a strenuous physical workout. Work with her to develop the tools to deal with her stress in a more positive way (see points 15 to 18).

Once you're educated about the dangers and realities of eating disorders, you will be able to intervene before your son or daughter develops medical problems. Seek professional medical and psychological help immediately, and if necessary, remove your child from the sport.

90. Approach weigh-ins with extreme caution

Some sports, like football and wrestling, have weight limitations for safety reasons. You don't want a 130-pound boy wrestling a 90-pound boy. That wouldn't be safe or fair. Because athletes in these sports compete in weight classes, they are required to weigh-in before matches. Weigh-ins, whether weekly or prior to competition, are common in other sports like gymnastics, figure skating, and track because leaner body mass is perceived to provide a competitive advantage. Coaches looking for the competitive edge in sports like soccer, basketball, and lacrosse are increasingly requiring weigh-ins as well.

Parents often ask me, "Do you think weigh-ins should be allowed in youth sports?"

There's no simple answer. In sports with weight classes, weigh-ins are unavoidable. If your son is a wrestler or football player, you will have to decide if he can handle the weigh-in pressure. If you're seeing a sudden change in his energy level or if he seems to be avoiding food twenty-four to forty-eight hours before a weigh-in, that can be a red flag that he's using drastic measures, like starving himself, to maintain his weight.

While weigh-ins in other sports can be a positive motivator for some kids to maintain a healthy weight, I think the potential for a negative impact to a child's self-esteem, especially for kids in the twelve- to seventeen-year-old range when body consciousness is particularly acute, outweighs the benefits. In a culture that so prizes lean body mass, it's a lot to ask of a kid to take the positive and leave the negative. You may say, "If you lose five pounds you'll be able to run faster," but kids hear,

"You're not good enough the way you are," and "I'll approve of you more when you're thinner."

I do not support charting weigh-ins and displaying the results for any sport. It's one thing to require athletes to cope with weigh-ins weekly or prior to competition, it's quite another to post the results on the locker room wall. This is a pressure tactic that leads to shame and humiliation. Shannon, a sixteen-year-old gymnast put it this way:

> *Every Monday we had to weigh-in and Coach would post the results on the wall where everyone could see. If you gained weight, he circled your name in red. If your name was in red, you would get teased by the other girls. They would say, "Shannon must have eaten a lot of doughnuts again." I used to want to die when my name was circled. I felt like I wasn't as good as the others. I started not eating as much over the weekend. Monday mornings, I would be starving but skip breakfast because it was easier than getting picked on and feeling worthless.*

Before you allow your child to play on a team where he or she is required to weigh-in on a regular basis, i.e., weekly or before every game, you should take the following steps:

- **Talk to your child's coach about his or her attitudes about weight, body fat, and performance.** Ask questions like, "Are the girls required to weigh-in?" "Do you believe that my son has to be a certain weight in order to perform?" and "What do you tell the team about their weight and performance?" If you suspect your child's coach is pressuring her to be thin, you should talk to the coach about it. You can say, "Help me understand why you think Arianna will perform better if she loses weight" or "Help me understand why you think Ben needs to lose seven pounds." Hear the coach out and then explain that you're concerned about eating disorders. Let him or her know that, "We need to be careful about what messages we send Arianna about her weight. I don't want her to think she's overweight and that we don't approve of how she looks."

- **Talk to your daughter about the dangers and realities of weight loss.** Let her know that even if she loses seven pounds and is able to compete better, it doesn't mean she needs to be thinner than that or that her body was undesirable or unhealthy before. Tell her that if she becomes too thin, she will be weak and unable to compete. Be honest about your concerns. Find out how she feels about being asked to lose weight. Ask her, "How did it make you feel when Coach asked you to lose seven pounds?" If she admits that it made her feel bad, ashamed, or unattractive, you will need to counteract that message with positive ones like, "You are attractive, no matter what your weight" and "Beautiful women come in all shapes and sizes." Don't deny her feelings by saying, "I don't want to hear you talk that way." Instead, validate her feelings by empathizing with her. You can say, "I understand why you might feel unattractive. Our society makes us feel like we need to be thin in order to be attractive. But it's not true. Let's look at some pictures of women athletes who are well built and strong."

- **Ask yourself, "Is my child ready to compete at this level?"** It may be a lot to ask a fourteen-year-old girl or boy to lose or gain ten pounds in order to compete. You may decide that this is simply asking too much. Some parents believe that the extra strength training and conditioning requirements that are also put upon athletes are too much. This doesn't mean you feel that your boy or girl is fragile or delicate, but if he's being asked to shed pounds or bulk up, then he's competing on a more demanding level. Include your child in any decision that you make, but ultimately, you're the parent and you have to make the tough calls in the best interest of your child. You may decide that she's too young or not in a good emotional place to meet the demands of competition. You may find that when she's older, more experienced, and has a more grounded self-image that changing her weight in order to compete is something she can safely handle.

91. Warn your child about the dangers of performance-enhancing drugs and supplements

The good news for parents when it comes to steroid use among athletes is that the word is out—steroids have dangerous side effects. Anabolic steroids, which are male hormones, can cause mood disorders, liver and heart damage, increase in aggressiveness, and sexual dysfunction. This new knowledge means that it's harder to use steroids without getting caught and the government and sports associations are campaigning to raise awareness among young athletes that steroids are harmful.

The bad news is that use of steroids and over-the-counter performance-enhancing supplements like creatine, the side effects of which are unknown, are on the rise, particularly among boys ages thirteen and older. Though normally considered a boy's problem, steroid use is fast becoming a negative trend among young female athletes as well. A recent Pennsylvania State University study showed that more young girls are abusing anabolic steroids in an effort to build strength while trimming fat. The nationwide study found that as many as 175,000 high school girls—about 1.4 percent of girls in ninth to twelfth grades—up from 0.4 percent in 1991—reported steroid use at least once in their lives. The report attributes the trend to the growing numbers of girls in competitive sports, greater competition for athletic scholarships, and more Olympic and professional opportunities for female athletes.

At the core of performance-enhancing drug use are self-esteem and body-image issues. Boys often believe that if they can develop superior athletic skills they will be more accepted and admired, and will feel better about themselves. And often, when they do have superior athletic skills, they are more popular. This makes the lure of steroid use hard to resist for many boys who crave recognition and acceptance. Girls often crave the lean, muscular body type that is difficult to obtain through diet and exercise alone. They think that if they have it, they will be more attractive and desirable.

Today's supercompetitive sports environment lends itself to performance-enhancing drug use. Some young people want to win at sports, no matter what the cost. They don't see beyond the here and now. They feel invincible. Teenagers simply don't think about the health consequences of taking drugs to perform better. It's the "It won't happen to me," syndrome. Because steroids and some supplements are known to enhance performance and the side effects are often delayed, it's much easier to dismiss the health risks. To complicate matters, several former baseball players have recently stated that steroids continue to be used by major league baseball players. Boys hear this and think, "Well, it can't be that bad" or "It must be safe, if he's doing it."

Tony was a track athlete who admitted to me that he started taking steroids when he was sixteen. Intellectually he knew they were dangerous, but emotionally, he wanted to win and he wanted to run track in college. "Being on steroids helped me train harder," Tony said, "so I felt like I wasn't cheating." Tony is now out of college and suffers from mood swings and shrunken testicles as a result of his steroid use.

Fortunately, parents can have a positive influence over their children when they take the following seven steps:

- **Educate your child.** Start a dialogue with your child when he or she is ten or eleven years old, before kids will feel the pressure to use steroids. When you hear about athletes using steroids in the media, use this as a jumping off point to talk about it. Spell out the health risks, especially that it can cause testicles to shrink or interfere with normal menstruation. Talk about football legend Lyle Alzado who attributed his fatal brain cancer and numerous other health problems to steroid use.

- **Talk about the consequences of cheating.** Sports is supposed to "Let the best man or woman win." Anyone who uses performance-enhancing drugs in any sport besides baseball is considered a cheater. Let your child know that famous athletes, like track star Ben Johnson, have been disqualified from performing in the Olympics because of steroid use. Though many athletes rationalize its use by saying, "If my competitors are using drugs, then I will be at an unfair disadvantage if I don't," it still means you're cheating. Though it can take a long time to sink in, tell your child, "You have to play with your God-given talents and see what you can make of yourself. If you don't make the college team or win the championship then at least you will be able to look at yourself in the mirror and know that you did it the right way." Though this may strike you as a cliché, if you are consistent in communicating this positive message to your children, and if you lead by positive example by not cheating yourself, it can become their philosophy.

- **Take a zero-tolerance stand.** You need to make it clear to your son or daughter that, "Taking steroids, or a performance-enhancing supplement like creatine, is something we won't tolerate." Be clear about the consequences, such as, "If we find out you're taking anything to enhance your performance, we will pull you from the team and you won't be allowed to play for the rest of the season."

- **Be familiar with the signs of steroid use.** Steroids can be taken as a pill or injected. If your son has a sudden growth spurt or suddenly seems bigger and more muscular to you, or your daughter starts losing her hair, her voice deepens, and/or her breasts shrink, steroids may be the cause. A sudden burst of facial hair, dramatic changes in mood, and changes in eating habits can also mean your son or daughter is taking steroids. Kids refer to steroids as "rocket fuel," "roids," or "juice."

- **Assume that no performance-enhancing supplement is safe.** Just because it's legal and sold in health food stores or over the Internet, doesn't mean it's safe. Supplements like creatine, which is a combination of amino acids, may be dangerous for a growing body. The research has yet to reach a conclusion about the safety of natural supplements.

- **Don't rely on your child's coach to spot the problem.** A college football coach said to me, "I have eighty players to keep track of and a limited amount of time. I can't be a mother hen to each and every one." It is hard to keep track of a team of players. While most coaches would never encourage steroid use, many are simply not trained to deal with the problem. And if a coach suspects his star player of using steroids, he may not want to deal with the problem head on and risk losing his best player. Though many coaches will work with parents in dealing with this issue, you can't assume that your child's coach will spot the problem and bring it to your attention.

• **Get professional help.** Your boy or girl will need to be evaluated by a medical professional as well as a counselor. A counselor can help deal with any of the mood-altering effects of steroid use as well as help your child deal with any self-esteem issues that may have led him or her to try to win, no matter what the cost.

Though the thought of their child using steroids is frightening, parents who take an early proactive approach to prevention are often successful.

92. Help athletically gifted athletes feel comfortable in the limelight

Most people assume that athletically gifted athletes are full of confidence and have high self-esteem. How could they not be with so many people cheering them on?

Often, just the opposite is true. Superstar athletes may be in the limelight, but the limelight isn't always an easy place to be. Chris, a sixteen-year-old basketball player, was considered one of the best high school players in the state. He was almost always the high scorer on his team. His picture was frequently in the local newspaper. He was his coach's star player. The principal and teachers patted him on the back.

However, since he gained notoriety, his two best friends, who were not on the team, called him less. They stopped coming to the games to cheer him on. Chris's parents contacted me after his game started to slide mid-season. He was sleeping and eating less. He wasn't consciously trying to screw up his game, but he knew that his friends were jealous of the attention he was receiving, and so he wasn't playing to his full ability. He thought that if didn't play as well his friends would like him again. I've seen this kind of problem quite a bit in boy and girl superstars. Because acceptance is so important to kids, especially in the teen years, they don't want to stand out from the other members of the team. However, when a gifted child denies his gifts in order to fit in with his peers, he often develops emotional problems like anxiety and depression.

I told Chris that he wasn't alone. Many gifted athletes have issues with friends and siblings. I routinely work with professional and Olympic athletes who have to deal with jealousy. I explained to him that even though we're happy when our friends are in the spotlight, there is often a part of us that wishes we were there too. We discussed Chris's options about whether he should discuss the problem with his friends. Chris decided he would say:

It really sucks that I don't get to hang out with you guys as much anymore. Any chance you can come to my game tomorrow? I play better when I know you're there making faces at me.

Chris and I then discussed how he would handle their reaction. If his friends decided to come, Chris would just let them know he was "psyched." If they told him they didn't want to or couldn't make the game, Chris was going to invite them to a movie. If they rejected that offer, Chris would simply say, "Okay, why don't you guys call me when you're free," and let it go.

The idea of letting his friends go was painful to Chris, but he was beginning to understand that not being himself was ultimately more painful. Sometimes, superstar athletes lose their friends. It's a painful reality of being talented. Talented kids need the courage to stand out. Mom and Dad play a big role in helping kids tap into their source of inner strength. If you're the parent of an athletically gifted child, be sure to:

- **Discuss the importance of being gracious.** It's great to be gifted, but it's not okay for kids to act like they're better than others. Teach your child to say, "Thank you," when given a compliment. Encourage her to talk about the team rather than herself: "We all played 100 percent" or "I had a lot of help out there. This is a great team." Keep your routine at home normal. Just because

Jasmine is the best lacrosse player in the county doesn't mean she gets out of doing the dishes.

- **Talk about the importance of not holding back in order to fit in.** Let him know that his relationships may change, but it's important for him to be accepted for who he is.

- **See your child as a whole person.** I've found that gifted athletes who are arrogant and act full of themselves often are the ones with the biggest self-esteem issues. These are the kids that feel pressured because their identity gets so wrapped up in being a star athlete that the thought of losing their status is unbearable. They therefore put on this arrogant front to fool themselves and others. When you see your child as a whole person and not just an athlete you can alleviate some of the pressure she may feel. You enable her to derive her identity from a variety of sources. It's especially important to talk to superstars about their accomplishments or interests outside of sports. A gifted college swimmer I know told me that she appreciates that her parents don't ask her about her sport immediately after saying hello. "They'll ask me about school and the fund-raiser I'm working on. Eventually, they'll ask me how it's going with my coach, but I really appreciate that they don't treat me as 'the swimmer.' "

93. Understand why your child is attracted to action or alternative sports

Your son starts saying things like, "I can do a 180 backslide just like Tony Hawk," and you're thinking what and who? Your daughter thinks Shannon Dunn is the coolest snowboarder she's ever seen and you didn't even know snowboarding was considered a sport.

Many young people are now attracted to action or alternative sports like snowboarding, skateboarding, rock climbing, and downhill bike racing. Kids find these sports appealing because of the independence and the elements of danger and risk inherent in these sports. Boys and girls are attracted to the more unstructured nature of these sports after playing structured sports like soccer, football, and hockey. In fact, it's the highly structured and organized nature of traditional youth sports that has, in part, fueled the popularity of the nontraditional ones. There is less adult participation and supervision in action sports. Kids feel nonconformist and rebellious by participating in these sports and that gives them a self-esteem boost.

But is this kind of self-esteem boost good for kids? It depends. What can be so unappealing to parents about these action sports is exactly what draws children of all ages to them: the danger, the risk, and, sometimes, the accompanying lifestyle and subculture, with its own language and clothing.

However, it's undeniable that these sports require athletic talent and courage. Being competent and brave enough to speed down a winding dirt hill at thirty miles an hour while maintaining balance and control will give kids a self-esteem boost. How could you not feel good about yourself after successfully completing a daring feat like that? Kids are also required to advance themselves through the sport. They must take on the responsibility for acquiring new skills and for practicing. Parents tell me things like, "Darren could never make it to soccer practice on time, but he's very committed and self-motivated in snowboarding." Some independent-minded kids do find their niche in action sports. When they love what they're doing and get the high from going against the grain kids do feel good about themselves.

But riding down a winding dirt hill at thirty miles an hour is inarguably dangerous. I don't know if I would want to watch one of my kids doing such a stunt. I understand why parents are concerned about action sports, but if you immediately dismiss the idea of your daughter mountain biking because it's too dangerous, you could end up fueling her desire and she will participate behind your back.

Instead of beginning a power struggle with your boy or girl over action sports, try to understand the root of her interest. The most important thing is to understand what draws your child to an action or extreme sport. Does she want to race on a mountain bike because she loves the challenge or because she thinks it will make her look cool? Are his friends pressuring him to ride his skateboard in the street or is he genuinely attracted to the more unstructured nature of skateboarding? Talk to your child and ask questions like, "Why do you love mountain biking? What do you get out of it?" You may discover that your child feels true passion about an action sport. In that case, you may decide to try to work with him to ensure his safety.

When Wanda took her thirteen-year-old daughter to a downhill biking competition, she was astonished to see women competing and many girls in the audience. She was also relieved to see that all participants wore helmets and other safety gear.

When they get to know about the action sport, some parents discover that the lifestyle that goes with the sport is not unhealthy or unsavory. One mom said she thought only unintelligent boys surfed because that was her stereotypical image of a surfer, a goofy kid who cut school to catch waves. "But once I got to know Brian's friends, I was impressed," she said. "They're all smart boys who do well in school. They don't cut classes and I don't think any of them do drugs."

If you make an effort to learn about a sport and why it's appealing to him, your child is less likely to feel dismissed or unheard. This sets the stage for a continuing dialogue rather than arguments and rebellion.

If you feel like your daughter is pursuing an action sport for the wrong reasons, such as to impress others or to rebel, you need to help her boost her self-esteem in other ways discussed in this section. If you feel your boy or girl has a self-esteem problem that seems beyond your help you may want to consider seeking professional help.

94. Support your child's identity quest—even if it takes him or her away from sports

When kids are in elementary school, they usually play sports because Mom and Dad signed them up. When kids are in middle school, they often want to play because their friends play. When kids are in high school, however, they play sports because they choose to play. A seven-year-old usually goes along with what Mom or Dad says. A fourteen-year-old girl, on the other hand, is going to have her own ideas about how she wants to spend her time. It may be in sports, but it may not.

Like Ashanti. As a young girl between the ages of seven and twelve, Ashanti always played softball and volleyball. She seemed to have such a good sense of herself—until she became a teenager. At fourteen, she lost interest in sports. Much to her parents' dismay, hanging out with her friends at the mall became her favorite pastime.

Raymond was a passionate soccer player up until the age of fifteen. Suddenly he announced that he wanted to play basketball. His parents worried that his lack of commitment to soccer would eventually translate to basketball and to other areas of his life.

Stories like Ashanti's and Raymond's are common. You may be disappointed to see your daughter leave a sport when she becomes a teenager. You may have put a lot of time, money, and energy into nurturing your son in a sport only to discover that he wants to play a new one. Your daughter may have worked really hard at soccer but now her commitment to the sport has lessened. The reality is that as your children grow, their true identity begins to form and their interests may shift;

their desire to play a certain sport or sports altogether may change.

Adolescence, the years between twelve and seventeen, is a critical time of identity development for kids. Though it can be upsetting to parents when kids want to back away from a sport or leave sports altogether, the key for parents is to remember that kids need to find out who they are in the world. This is normal, healthy, and to be expected. What parents might see as a "lack of commitment," is often a "shift in commitment," as their boy or girl explores other sports or interests outside of sports.

I ask parents, "Would you prefer that your daughter not open her eyes to the world?" or "Is it better for your son to be a soccer-playing machine throughout his adolescence or for him to truly discover his true passion?" I understand a parent's concern about a daughter hanging out at the mall or a son's lack of enthusiasm for any activity. It's ironic that at the age when kids most need the empowering and self-esteem-boosting benefits that sports can offer, often is the age when many kids turn away from sports. However, as I discussed in the chapter on quitting (chapter 8) there are many valid reasons kids have for choosing not to play a sport. And most important, you can't force a child to play a sport if he or she doesn't want to play it. Denying your child's interests or not allowing your kid to discover what those interests are can be far more damaging to your child's self-esteem in the long run than not playing a sport. It's as if you're saying, "I don't trust you to figure out who you really are" or "We like you best as the tennis player we want you to be, not as the skateboarder you tell us you want to be."

What you can do is provide support and guidance for your children as they pursue their identity. You can do this by:

- **Figuring out what level of sports participation will work for her.** If your daughter wants to leave track the question you want to ask is not, "How can we get Ashanti to stay on the track team?" but "Can she reduce her commitment to the sport but still participate and get some benefit out of running track?" Just because she's not going to be a state champion or run track in college doesn't mean she can't still run a respectable time in the five-hundred meters. She can practice less and thereby have more time and energy to explore other interests. She will stay active and healthy. She will still be a part of her team. It's worth encouraging (but not forcing) your child to downsize before leaving a sport altogether. She still needs to commit to attending practice, being on time, and working hard when she's there.

- **Evaluating your expectations.** When parents tell me, "Joey quit baseball and now he doesn't want to do any-thing," I wonder if Joey just doesn't want to do what they want him to do. If that's not the case, I wonder what kinds of expectations Joey's parents have for him. If your expectations are too great for your son—for example, that he play a sport, take piano lessons, get all A's and B's in school, and do his chores without being asked, he may shut down and withdraw from his nor-mal activities. At the critical time when he's trying to fig-ure out who he is, he can start to think that measuring up to your expectations to be good at everything is too hard. Very few people are good at everything. And if it's hopeless, why bother trying at all? This is a general kind of burnout that kids under too much pressure in one or more areas of their lives experience. When your approach is, "I want my child to find out what gives him joy and what he loves doing," which will give him a true sense of self, rather than, "I want him to do everything well," kids feel like they have the space to explore and try new things.

- **Acknowledging your loss.** It's normal for you to be disappointed if your child loses her enthusiasm or passion for a sport. It doesn't mean you were living through her experiences or that you crossed a line. It means you're being honest about how you feel. And that's okay as long as your child's needs are on the front burner and yours are on the back burner. Being sad that Jamie isn't going to play basketball in college because you always dreamed of sitting in the stands and cheering her on is understandable. What you don't want to do is to try to force Jamie to play basketball because it's what you want. It's better for parents to be open about how they feel than to hide it. Your child may otherwise sense your loss and feel guilty or disapproved of. Talk to your child and let him know your point of view. For example you can say, "I understand that you're tired of ice skating and want to try lacrosse. It's just that I enjoyed traveling with you every weekend and being with all of the other parents. I'm going to need some time to let that go."

I know it can take a leap of faith for parents to let their children back away from sports, but I have seen many thirteen-and fourteen-year-olds back away only to return in two or three years. When kids are allowed to explore their identity and ultimately decide, "Yes, I want to play soccer," they're in a better position to make a commitment.

X

. . . .

FAMILY ISSUES:

Work together in the best interest of your children—and respect your own needs

Good communication between sports parents is essential but not always easy. Divorced parents may find themselves even more challenged to reach the right decisions for their sports-playing children. And single parents have their own set of sports-parenting issues. But no matter what the family situation, there are strategies that can help moms and dads work together to effectively parent their children in sports.

95. Keep the lines of communication open with your child's other parent

Jesus was a fourteen-year-old basketball player who was show-ing great promise. But his mother felt that he spent too much time playing basketball and not enough time pursuing other activities, like art and academics. "What is Jesus going to do if he doesn't get picked to play in college? And even if he does, the chances that he'll make the pros are so slim. What will he do then?" she asked.

Jesus's dad, on the other hand, was thrilled that his son was so into basketball. "I was a good athlete and I know it helped me feel better about myself," he said. "Jesus really has a shot to play in college."

These parents were unable to discuss the subject of Jesus's ball playing without erupting into a bitter argument.

"I hate when my parents fight about me," Jesus told me. "It makes me feel like I'm doing something bad or messing them up. I don't want them to get divorced over me."

Your child isn't the only person you need to communi-cate with when it comes to sports. Dads and moms, regard-less of their marital status, need to have good communica-tion, too. It can be especially difficult for children when par-ents argue about sports issues concerning them. Kids worry that fighting parents will divorce and they feel guilty to be the source of the conflict. They think, "I must be doing something wrong for Mom and Dad to fight like this." It's important for parents to calmly discuss and come to an agreement about any issues related to their child's sports playing.

Here are four steps you can take to communicate better with your child's other parent about sports:

- **Be clear about what you need from the other parent.** Sometimes I just need my wife to listen to me about our children's sports. But Debbie is not a mind reader. So I tell her, "I just need you to listen to me. I don't need any feedback from you. I just need to blow off some steam because the ref made a bad call against Eli." There are other times when I need her advice or her help in moving on, as in, "Tell me I'm overreacting and I need to get over the bad call." This works in reverse. Sometimes Debbie just needs me to listen or she needs advice. By being clear about what we need from each other, we avoid arguments and misunderstandings.

- **Avoid labeling the other parent's behavior.** When Jen and Gerry walked into my office, Jen immediately pointed to her husband and said, "He's a total nut case about Jack's rowing. You have to help him." Though she didn't mean any harm, Jen labeled Gerry and by doing so, she was disrespectful of his point of view. Sports was emotional and important to him. Instead, she put him on the defensive by calling him a "nut." Instead of communicating about their son's rowing, Gerry had to defend himself, "I'm not a nut case and I resent you calling me that!" Labeling is common between sports parents. One man accused his wife of being, "The World's most obsessive soccer mom," because she never missed a practice or a game. As it turned out, this dad felt guilty for not participating on the same level as his wife did and he made fun of her to cover his own guilt. Respect the other parent's point of view and opinions by not labeling or judging. It is almost impossible to have healthy communication with someone who is calling you a nut or accusing you of losing your mind about sports.

- **Bridge the gap in understanding.** If your husband thinks that you are too involved in your son's baseball career because you yell on the sidelines and argue with the umpires, try to help him understand your point of view. Of course, this means you will have to understand why sports is so emotional for you. As I say in the Awareness chapter (chapter 1), understanding what memories, emotions, or fears motivate your behavior is the cornerstone of successful sports parenting. You can then say, "When I was growing up, no one ever paid attention to my sports activities. I always went to games alone. There was no one there to stick up for me and I don't want that to happen to Thomas." Or if you don't understand why your husband sulks and stews when your son doesn't catch a baseball, ask him, "Help me to understand why you get so upset when Thomas drops a ball during a game." When you understand each other's attitudes and emotional issues about sports, you will be better able to work toward a solution, like "You're a great mom. I know you don't want Thomas to feel that we don't care about his sports. But do you see how when you argue with the umpire, Thomas gets embarassed?"

- **Agree to disagree if necessary.** You don't have to see eye to eye on your child's sports issue in order to have good communication. If you understand the other person's point of view and he understands yours, you can agree to disagree. You may decide to set some boundaries in behavior. For example, Jen can't label Gerry "A nut case," but Gerry isn't allowed to yell on the sidelines or talk about sports at dinner. It's rare that parents will agree 100 percent on what's best for the child. The important thing is to reach a mutual understanding so you don't have a source of conflict always brewing between you.

96. Negotiate with your ex-spouse in the best interest of your child

Kim is a sixteen-year-old diver who was to receive a prestigious award. Her mother, because she drove Kim to all of her lessons and attended most of her competitions, felt that she should be the parent to attend the ceremony. Yet Kim's father, because he lived in another city and missed out on her day-to-day activities, wanted to make a special trip to attend.

They asked Kim, "Who do want to go with you?"

Kim said, "Don't make me choose. I want you both."

Unfortunately, Kim's mom refused to attend when her ex-husband insisted upon bringing his new fiancée. In the end, Kim's older brother went with her to the ceremony.

All too often, a child's sporting activities become yet another arena for conflict between divorced parents. In the same way divorce affects the division of responsibilities—who takes Juan to his dentist appoints, and who gets the kids for the holidays—sports is another area that divorced parents need to negotiate.

Often parents do what Kim's mom and dad did; they ask the child to choose. While I think it's important for parents to discuss their decisions with their children, I don't think it's appropriate to put the burden of choice on the child. Many children already feel guilty and responsible for their parents' problems. Asking a child to choose one parent over another makes a kid feel even more guilty and confused. Children don't want to hurt either parent's feelings and yet making a choice forces them to do just that.

Instead of putting your child in the middle, negotiate with your ex-spouse and then talk to your child about why you reached your decision. For example, "Laurie, we've decided that your father will take you to the soccer banquet because he's missed so much all year long."

Of course, Laurie's mother could easily take the position that her ex-husband doesn't deserve to go to the award ceremony because he didn't put any time into nurturing their daughter in soccer. She would even be justified because she is the parent in the day-to-day trenches. But at these moments parents need to step back and ask themselves, "Is my anger going to be good for Laurie or bad for her? Is this about me or about her?"

When working out your custody arrangement, consider the importance and continuity of sports in your child's life. When you're deciding who will see your child on which weekend and where, consider the impact on your child's sporting life. A boy on my son's baseball team had to stop playing because he spent every other weekend three hours away with his father. This boy was crushed to give up baseball. Not only were his parents separating, which was traumatic in itself, he also had to give up his favorite activity and the friends he had made. I understand that there are times when it is necessary to disrupt a child's sporting life, but I also believe that many parents can negotiate a solution if they set aside their differences and work together in the best interest of the child. I know a couple who change their custody arrangement every fall and winter so their son can stay on the football team. They do this because football is important to the boy and they want him to have the continuity of being on his team.

When separated or divorced parents are able to make decisions about who will pay for Scott's new hockey equipment and who will go to Jessica's big lacrosse game purely with the best interest of the child in mind, they avoid the unfortunate trap that so many divorced couples fall into—making sports yet another area of conflict. Divorced parents who work together on sports issues find that it has a positive impact on their child.

97. Find ways to stay involved, even if you're far away or have other priorities

Ralph had to take a job in another city and couldn't attend his son Hector's swim meets. Allison is a single mom who needs to work two jobs to keep her family going. She would love to be able to take her children to their practices and watch their games, but she simply doesn't have the time.

Many parents today find themselves in similar situations. Financial or other demands make it impossible for them to be present for their children's sporting activities on a regular basis. But there are ways to stay involved and show your interest. Here are four ideas:

- **Be honest.** Talk to your child about why you can't be there on a regular basis. You can say, "There's nowhere I'd rather be than at your tennis match, but I have to work in order to support our family. Sometimes, we have to make sacrifices that don't make us happy but that we know are good in the long run." Or you can just offer her the reassurance that, "Though I'm not going to be at your game physically, I'm thinking about you and rooting for you all the time."

- **Set aside a specific time each day to talk about sports with your child.** No matter how busy Allison is, she makes it a point to get up a half an hour early so she can have breakfast with her kids. This is her time for asking her son how his soccer practices are going and for finding out if her daughter is getting along better with her field hockey coach. Parents who live in separate cities can schedule a nightly phone call with their child to find out how baseball or gymnastics is going.

- **Videotape a game.** A single mom asked me to videotape our daughters' volleyball match because she couldn't be there. She gave me the camera and showed me how to use it. I was happy to do this for her. I know of other parents who do this and send the tape to the other parent if they don't live in the same city.

- **Find out what's most important to your child.** If you can only attend one game of the season, ask your child which one she would like it to be. You might think she wants you to be at the big game at the end of the season but she might surprise you by letting you know she would prefer you to be at the first game. Asking her what's most important will show her that you care about her feelings and preferences.

Though it's not the same as being there, expressing your interest by asking, "How did the game go?" or "How did you play today?" and taking the time to listen to the answers will go a long way in bridging the gap of your physical absence.

98. Reach out for help if you're a single parent

Because of time constraints, it can be difficult for single parents to be as involved in their children's sporting lives as they may like.

Single moms may also have the added complication of having no or limited experience with sports themselves. They grew up at a time when sports opportunities for girls were still limited. Now they find themselves parenting boys and girls who are active in sports.

If you're a single parent and you have sports-playing children, don't be shy about reaching out to others for help. You can't do it all alone. Though your time and energy may be limited, there are ways for you to get help in nurturing your child's athletic interests:

- **Find sports mentors for your child.** When Kathy's son showed an early interest in basketball, she knew she lacked the coordination and know-how to help her son build his skills. She asked a neighbor she trusted to help him practice after dinner and to go to games. Her neighbor was only too happy to help. Extended family members, friends, and neighbors can be invaluable sports mentors. Some organizations, like Big Brothers, Big Sisters may also be able to help you find a sports mentor for your child. You may want to recruit more than one sports mentor. Consider what each one has to offer and what your child needs. One may be particularly knowledgeable in sports while another may be good at offering encouragement.

- **Get a sports mentor for yourself.** It can be helpful to have another parent, friend, or family member with sports experience in your corner. You can ask this person for guidance and information when you need it. For example, you may want to know if your child has a natural talent for the game or what his statistics mean. Or you may have a question like, "William seems nervous before his games, is this normal?" "I've never dealt with a coach before. Does she seem like she knows what she's doing?" or "How many practices should I try to go to?" Having guidance and support will build your confidence as a sports parent.

- **Ask other parents for help.** At the beginning of the season, most coaches give out the names and phone numbers of the other parents. If your child's coach doesn't, ask him or her for the information. Call the other parents to arrange for rides to practices if that's a problem. One single mom asked her son's teammate's father to watch out for him at games and to let her know if there were any problems.

99. Don't assume that you have to have a male figure in your child's sporting life

Many single mothers, whether never married, divorced, or widowed, worry that their children must have a male influence in order to be successful in sports. This simply isn't true. What your child needs is the appropriate resources, practice, encouragement, and knowledge to succeed in sports. There are many children who are successful in sports whose dads don't play or aren't interested in sports. A friend of my son is a talented athlete and his father will be the first to tell you that he is not athletic and doesn't even have much interest in sports. Through my work at sports camps, I have met hundreds of fatherless boys and girls who have terrific athletic skills and self-confidence.

If you're a single mother concerned about the lack of a father to nurture your sports-playing child, you can take these three steps:

- **Have a positive attitude.** Don't lament, "Well, I can't help you with your soccer because I don't have the time or the know-how. If your dad was around, he would help you, but he's not." Your child may end up believing that he can't get the needed help. He may end up feeling that it's hopeless to pursue sports. If on the other hand, you are positive and say, "We have a lot of terrific resources to help you with your passing skills," your child will feel positive and hopeful too.

- **Encourage your child to learn sports from a variety of sources.** Kids don't just learn about sports from one person. Your child will have a variety of coaches, gym teachers, peers, camps, and clinics.

- **Find a male mentor if and when your child needs one.** Don't assume or believe that your child must have a male sports mentor in order to be successful, but if that's what she needs, then make that happen. A widowed mom chose to have her eight-year-old daughter taken to her softball games by an uncle even though an aunt with a lot of softball experience was available. She felt that her daughter would benefit from the continuity of having a man take her to her sporting events because her own father had always played that role. If your twelve-year-old son tells you, "I wish I had a dad to play ball with," then I would find a male sports mentor for him. Keep in mind, he may want a male figure around not just to play catch with but because his identity is forming and he wants a role model for other areas of life as well. What your children need changes as they age and develop. Be sensitive to their needs and do the best you can to find a male mentor if and when they need one.

A father figure can be helpful and positive for your child, especially when she asks for it or you sense that she needs it. It's not an absolute must. Your child can still develop her athletic skills or feel good about herself as an athlete without a male influence.

100. Don't fall into the guilt trap

Many single parents, whether never married, divorced, or widowed, feel the pressure to fill their own role as well as that of the missing parent. Many single parents feel guilty because they're not doing a better job or worry that their child is being cheated out of the other parent.

If you're feeling guilty, be aware that it can cloud your judgment and your decision-making ability when it comes to your child's athletic activities. Judy worked a full-time job with mandatory overtime and then an extra part-time job on the weekends because she couldn't say no to her son when he wanted to play baseball on the travel team. "I feel bad because he doesn't have a dad. I figure the least I can do is let him be on the travel team," she said. Guilt over being a single parent isn't an appropriate reason to make a decision about whether a child should play on a travel team. His readiness to compete at a higher level and what's best for the family overall should be the main factors in making this kind of important decision.

A single father indulged his daughter's dream of becoming a successful figure skater by allowing her to work with a private coach four times a week even though he thought it was unnecessary and the cost was great. "It's hard for me to tell Serena no. I want her to be happy and it's harder for her to be happy without a mom," he admitted.

If you're a single mom or dad parenting a child in sports, accept that you can't be both parents and that's okay. Most children grow up to lead happy and productive lives despite having only one parent. If you find yourself thinking, "I should be able to get to every one of Savannah's gymnastic competitions" or "I should be doing more to help Joey in fencing," remember that you're doing your best and that's all you can do. Try to leave the "shoulds" out of your thoughts.

Most of all, don't be afraid to say no when it's appropriate. If you can't afford to allow your son to play ice hockey, you shouldn't go into debt or take on another job. Sometimes kids have to hear, "I wish we could do this, but it's not going to happen." You can't compensate for the lack of another parent by indulging your child in sports or any other activity.

Believe that if you love your child and if you do your best to communicate that love through your words and your actions she will be happy and healthy, not in spite of having only one parent, but because the parent she did have made decisions for the right reasons.

101. Do what works for your entire family

With more kids specializing in one sport and playing year-round, the time, money, and energy that parents are expending can begin to take a toll on the family. Even kids who don't specialize but who play multiple sports can place a burden on Mom and Dad's resources. Some parents never get a break from the practices and games as their child moves from outdoor to indoor play. If your child is on a traveling team, the sacrifice in time and money is even more significant. Parents tell me all the time: "I feel like we have no life outside of our kids' sporting activities."

That's a big problem. While sports can provide a terrific opportunity for kids to have fun and develop lifelong skills, these benefits are undermined when parents make too huge an investment in their children's sports careers. A fourth grader doesn't need a personal trainer and a fifth grader doesn't need a shooting coach. Treating sports as the top family priority can drain a family's resources and energy. I'm a proponent of kids playing multiple sports year-round, but it has to make sense and work for the entire family. If you have two or more kids playing multiple sports, you may have to draw the line and say, as Terry did, "You can each play two sports a year because any more than that is too much of a strain."

To focus family life so heavily around a seventh grader's soccer schedule—to give up vacations to go to tournaments and never to have time together on weekends, can have negative consequences for the whole family. Parents burn out, siblings feel resentful, and communication on nonsports matters suffers.

Because Mom and Dad want to provide their children with

the opportunity to develop their athletic skills and follow their dreams, it can be difficult to say no when a child wants to play organized sports all year-round. As I discuss in the Specialization chapter (chapter 4), many parents worry that their children will somehow fall terribly behind in athletic development. This worry and this fear are what the parents focus on instead of how they really feel about the toll sports is taking on them personally and the family in general.

Just as children exhibit stress and signs of depression and anxiety because of their sports participation, Mom and Dad can too. If you find yourself feeling exhausted all the time, always running behind, never having any time for yourself, or unnaturally short-tempered, you may need a break from sports. I recommend you do the following:

- **Track how much time you're actually spending on sporting activities.** Get a calendar and write it down. If you have more than one child, use different color markers or highlighters. Many parents are stunned to discover how much time their child's sport takes up when they actually see it in black and white. One mom showed me her calendar and remarked, "No wonder I feel like I have no life. I don't!" Once she saw how much time her son's hockey and basketball were sucking up, she knew it was time for a change.

- **Keep a record of all the nonsporting events or family togetherness that you've missed.** Take a calendar and write in any activity or event, even if it's just relaxing or watching a favorite TV show, that you or the entire family had to miss because of a sports-related event. You may be surprised to discover all the activities that you are unable to do or enjoy because of a child's sports commitment.

- **Write a mission or vision statement for your family.** What activities would you like to do that you're not currently doing because you have no time outside of sports? What's most important to you as a family? Think about your priorities. Is it having fun together? Eating one meal together each day? One family decided that they missed playing board games together. So they instituted "game night" every Wednesday. If one child's sporting activities fell on that evening the child would miss that practice or game (unless it was a championship game) to be with the family. Once you've decided what's most important to you, honor it. Make the necessary cutbacks in your child's sporting schedule to make it happen.

- **Give yourself permission to take a break.** No, you will not be permanently damaging or cheating your child by not allowing him to play two seasons of soccer at age ten or to go to sports camp for six weeks this summer. If running your child to practices and games every night or every weekend is burning you out, take a season off. Your child can still stay active by walking to school, riding his bike, or playing with his friends.

Your child might not understand or appreciate your decision to cut back on sports, but in the long run it will benefit the entire family. I believe that what's good for Mom and Dad is ultimately good for the child. Sports is wonderful for both kids and parents when it's integrated into family life in a way that makes sense for everyone.

CONCLUSION

• • • • • • • • • • • • • • •

Creating positive memories for kids in sports

I'd like to share one last thought . . .

Last summer at a sports camp I work with, a group of thirteen- and fourteen-year-old boys were reminiscing about the good old days—for them it was the previous two summers. For about five minutes, they talked about scores and who won this and that championship. After that, they talked and laughed for over a half an hour about the time one of them slid into home base and ripped his pants, about getting chased off the field by a swarm of bees, about who ran the wrong way on the soccer field, and about the time they dumped ice water over their favorite coach's head.

As I listened to them, it occurred to me how little time they spent reflecting upon winning and scores. It reminded me of my own twenty-fifth high school reunion, when I stayed up half the night reminiscing with the guys from my old baseball team. We didn't talk about scores or standings. What mattered to us was what mattered to the boys at camp—the camaraderie, the fun, and the memorable events that had happened through sports play. I thought, "This is it. This is truly the ultimate reward when kids play sports. They create wonderful memories."

Think about it, the memories your child will create as she

plays sports will be with her forever. When your son is at his twenty-fifth high school reunion, he can gather with his old teammates and talk about the good old days, just as the boys at camp were doing. I can guarantee you, winning and losing won't be what they remember most. It will be the fun they had together.

If, as parents, we can remember that we are helping our children create positive memories about sports, memories that will last a lifetime, we will be less likely to make too much out of winning and losing. We will be able to keep perspective and to help our kids keep theirs. When we're not too worried about scores and standings, we can remember that what sports-playing kids need the most is to know that we love them win or lose. No matter what.

ACKNOWLEDGMENTS

How can I acknowledge all the family, friends, teachers, and colleagues I've had who, in their own way, have contributed to this book? After all, the feelings, thoughts, ideas, and 101 ways that I have expressed in this book are a compilation of my personal and professional life experiences.

I hope I've expressed my gratitude to all those in my life who have contributed to the writing of this book. If not, I will do my best to continue to do so.

Having said that, I would like to thank several individuals who have directly been an enormous help to me in this endeavor: Susan Magee has been the consummate professional and has been wonderful to work with. Her expertise, creativity, and writing ability are exceptional. Her caring and friendship, however, were equally important in our being able to complete this book.

David Fuqua, my friend and colleague, without whose help and wisdom I could not be doing professionally what I'm doing. In addition, without David, there is no way I would have been able to do the day-to-day work necessary to complete this book.

I want to thank Doris Cooper, my editor at Simon & Schuster, without whose guidance and support this project would not have been possible.

I would also like to thank my agent, Pam Bernstein, who believed in me and this book, and who guided me throughout the process of writing it.

Again, I will try my best to personally thank the other people in my life whose support has enabled me to complete this project. Writing it has personally been very fulfilling. Indeed, writing this book has been a pleasure.

ABOUT THE AUTHOR

DR. JOEL FISH is a licensed psychologist and a nationally recognized expert in sport psychology who has worked in the field for the past twenty years. He has worked extensively with athletes of all ages and skills levels, from youth sports through the Olympic and professional ranks. Dr. Fish has been a sport psychology consultant for the Philadelphia Flyers, 76ers, and Phillies organizations, and the USA Women's National Soccer Team. He has spoken nationwide on sport psychology at over 150 universities and is a popular presenter at a variety of athletic functions. Dr. Fish is currently the director of The Center For Sport Psychology in Philadelphia, Pennsylvania (www.psychologyofsport.com).

INDEX

action sports, 266–68
acute injuries, 180
adolescents, 4
  extra support needed by, 245–48
  identity development of, 233–34,
    270
  peer pressure and, xvi
  specialization by, 92–94, 105
alternative sports, 266–68
Alzado, Lyle, 260
American College of Sports
  Medicine, 97
American Pediatric Association, 97
anabolic steroids, 175, 258–62
anorexia, 251–52
aptitude, natural, 89–90
attention, gifted athletes' handling
  of, 263–65

biking, downhill, 267–68
binge eating, 251–53
Bird, Larry, 147
Bird, Sue, 9
body, rebuilding trust in, 193–94
body image, 242–44, 258–59
boys:
  eating disorders and, 249–53
  steroid use by, 258–59
breathing and relaxation, 44
bulimia, 251–53
burnout, 107–8, 114–16
  nonplaying seasons and, 117
  signs of, 115–16
bursitis, 180

calmness, 45–46
Centers for Disease Control and
  Prevention, 173
cheating, 260

children:
  and communicating with
    coaches, 132–35
  competitive stress and, see com-
    petition, competitive stress
  eating disorders and, 249–53
  energy levels of, 89
  giving unconditional love to,
    2–4, 13–14
  interest levels of, 88–89, 93,
    153–54, 206–7
  listening vs. talking to, 6–7
  mentors for, 283, 286
  natural aptitude and, 89–90
  parental communication with, see
    parent-child communication
  parents' identification with,
    19–20, 101
  personality of, 207
  positive mantras for, 41–42
  in recruitment process, 136–39
  self-esteem of, see self-esteem
  in sibling rivalries, see sibling
    rivalry
  skill levels of, 207, 236
  steroids and, 258–62
  see also adolescents; elementary
    school children; middle school
    children
"choking," 73–77
chronic injuries, 180, 195–96
coaches, 119–45
  adjusting to different styles of,
    115
  advocating for own child with,
    126–28
  authoritarian-style, 129–31
  communication by children with,
    132–35

Fish, Talia, v, xv, 16, 34, 64, 236, 239
frustration, dealing with, 208–11
girls:
eating disorders and, 249–53
steroid use by, 258
Title IX and, 102
Gretzky, Wayne, 21
guilt, parental, 287–88

Hamm, Mia, 242
Hawk, Tony, 266
healing, emotional aspects of, 190–92
high school adolescents, *see* adolescents
Hughes, Sarah, 104
hydration, 176

identity issues, 50
of adolescents, 233–34, 270
and importance of parental support, 269–72
and losing perspective in sports, 218
of middle school children, xv
specialization and, 97–98
see also self-esteem
injuries, 173–99
accurate articulation of, 186–87
acute, 180
annual number of, 173
chronic, 180, 195–96
coaches and, 183, 198
danger of playing through, 183–85
emotional aspects of healing after, 190–92
faking of, 188–89
most common types of, 173
precautionary guidelines for, 96, 174–76
rehabilitation process and, 183–84
researching of, 177–79
safe play after, 197–99

in sibling rivalries, 154
specialization and, 180–82
trusting the body after, 193–94
interest levels:
of children vs. adolescents, 93
and extra practice, 88–89
matching sports with, 206–7
and sibling rivalries, 153–54

jealousy:
of friends and classmates, 263–64
between siblings, 159–61
Johnson, Ben, 260
Johnson, Magic, 147
Jordan, Michael, 9, 106

knee injury, chronic, 180
Kwan, Michelle, 9

"ladders," in rebuilding trust in the body, 193–94
laxatives, 175
ligaments, sprained, 173

mantras:
for nervousness, 41–42
for parents' self-control, 28
memories, positive, 293–94
mentors:
for children, 283–84, 286
for parents, 284
middle school children, 4
competitive stress and, 65
identity issues and, xv, 269
quitting as option for, 204
specialization and, 95–96, 105–8
trophies and, 240–41
mothers, single, 283–86
muscle strain, 173

National Athletic Trainers' Association, 179
National Collegiate Athletic Association (NCAA), 136, 138
National Safe Kids Campaign, 174

snowboarding, 266
specialization, 91–118
  age level and, 92–94
  burnout and, 107–8, 114–16, 117
  drawbacks to, 104–8
  guidelines for, 95–96
  injuries and, 180–82
  nonplaying seasons and, 117–18
  physical and psychological
    impact of, 97–98
  reevaluation and, 111–13
  scholarships and, 102–3
  travel teams and, 109–10
  wrong reasons for, 99–101
sports:
  action or alternative, 266–68
  countering society's high value
    on, 235–39
  creating positive memories
    through, 293–94
  downside to, xi–xiii
  generational changes in, x–xi, 91,
    114
  long-term meaning of, xiii–xiv
  modifying parental involvement
    in, 27–28
  number of children involved in,
    ix, xii
  parent-child communication
    about, see parent-child com-
    munication
  parents emotionally affected by,
    16–18
  past histories of parents in,
    23–26
  personal goals of parents in, 25
  professional, 237
  reasons for playing of, 9–10
sportsmanship:
  parents as role models of, 29–30
  between siblings, 168–69
sprained ligaments, 173
steroids, 175, 258–62
strained muscles, 173

strength, safety and, 183
stress, see competition, competitive
  stress
stretching, 175
supplements, performance-
  enhancing, 258–62
surfing, 268

teams:
  not making of, 70–72
  post-injury involvement with,
    192
  removing child from, 142–43
  showing right way to leave to,
    230–31
  travel and, 109–10
tendonitis, 180
tension, physical effects of, 80
Title IX, 102
trophies, 239–41

unconditional love, 2–4, 13–14

Van Arsdale, Tom and Dick, 166
visualization exercises, 83–85

warming up, 175
weigh-ins, 254–57
weight loss, 175, 250, 256
weight training, 175
Williams, Venus and Serena,
  166–67
winning:
  assessing importance of, 21–22
  memories of moments other
    than, 293–94
  overemphasis on, xii–xiii, 3,
    9–10, 33
  see also competition, competitive
    stress
Woods, Tiger, 9, 33, 36, 104

Youth Sports Institute, xii, 97

302 • INDEX